EDUCATING FOR CHANGE

Implications for Business Education

by

Lucille Kornegay

DORRANCE PUBLISHING CO., INC.
PITTSBURGH, PENNSYLVANIA 15222

All Rights Reserved
Copyright © 2001 by Lucille Kornegay
No part of this book may be reproduced or transmitted
in any form or by any means, electronic or mechanical,
including photocopying, recording, or by any information
storage or retrieval system without permission in writing
from the publisher.

ISBN # 0-8059-5136-9
Printed in the United States of America

First Printing

For information or to order additional books, please write:
Dorrance Publishing Co., Inc.
643 Smithfield Street
Pittsburgh, Pennsylvania 15222
U.S.A.
1 800 788 7654
Or visit our web site and on-line catalog at *www.dorrancepublishing.com*

Dedication

To my daughter, Janice.

CONTENTS

Abstract vii

Introduction 1

    Overview 1
        Hypothesis 1
        The Problem 1

    Review of Related Literature 4
        Needs and Motivation 4
        Discovery Learning 6
        Piaget's Theory of Cognitive Development 7
        Technology/Experiential 10

    Historical Background 14
        Definition of Terms 15
        History of Machines 17
        Technological Development 17

Changing Needs and Reforms 22

    The Reform Movement 22

    Personal Inquires 24
        Cooperative Learning—Another Approach to Learning 28
        School Based Management 32
        Smaller is Better 35

    Political and Educational Reform 42
        Looking at School Reform 42
        Privatization and Choice 43
        Teacher Preparation and Reform 51
        Professional Development Schools 51
        Accountability in Education 53

Conclusion 55
    Curriculum Integration 55
    Educating With a Global Perspective 59
    Education and Technology 62
    The Challenge 64

Summary 67

Bibliography 69

Abstract

The survey conducted concludes that a small learning community in a comprehensive high school affords students an opportunity to become actively involved in the learning process. When students work in small groups, they articulate their own opinions, debate, and make decisions. Students learn how to learn.

Changes must occur in curricula and methods if educators are to prepare students to become lifelong learners who are equipped to meet the challenges that will face them in a competitive global society.

Technology holds great potential for the improvement of education and the delivery of educational services. Business educators are in a position to become advocates for change, which would include the integration of academic and vocational education.

INTRODUCTION

OVERVIEW

In *Megatrends 2000*, Naisbitt states, "As the world moves to a global economic society, human resources become the competitive edge for countries" (Naisbitt 1990). Educators must be aware of the changing society and accordingly, be willing to update, innovate, and propose new curricula and use teaching strategies that will provide students with skills that relate school to work.

Findings imply that business curricula and methods need to be reformed if teachers are to prepare students to become lifelong learners who are knowledgeable, skilled, and have the technical expertise to adapt to new technology. Major conclusions are in line with Bruner (1971), who emphasizes the importance of understanding the structure of a subject being studied, the need for active learning to make personal discoveries the basis for true understanding, and the value of inductive reasoning in learning.

Finally, technologies in most American schools have not kept pace with the larger society, and this deficiency must be improved. The challenge for business educators is to become the advocates for change and to provide the kind of leadership that will bring education into the twenty-first century.

Hypothesis

The education of the whole person involves two areas, theory and experience. It is evident from research that students must have hands-on experience that involves them in the process—the tasks and the theory. The more actively students are involved in the learning process and take personal responsibility for their learning outcomes, the greater the learning results.

The Problem

How can business educators develop the whole person to reach his or her potential through business technology? The focus will be on helping educators develop the human dimension in their students as they prepare them to be competent individuals who will become self-educating, lifelong learners.

There are three basic principles that will enhance the participation of the student. (1) All education must be relevant and linked to the background and drives of the student. (2) Education must be a hands-on, practical process. (3) Education must be appropriate for the cognitive stage of development of the individual for whom it is designed.

Educators must make all education relevant to life and work in a global society—a society made up of individuals whose roles largely consist of meeting the demands of the workplace.

Never before has society demanded so much of education. Not only must the educational institution adjust itself to our country's social forces, it must also respond to one of the major charges the American people have placed on schools: to provide each student with an education for individual excellence according to that student's a singular abilities. The kind of education today's student requires, therefore, is personal and unique.

The overriding trend affecting education at the beginning of the new millennium will certainly be the reduced probabilities of international conflict and the globalization of the economy.

In *Megatrends 2000*, John Naisbitt states, "As the world moves to a global economic society, human resources become the competitive edge for countries" (Naisbitt 1990).

Educational achievement is an aspect of a competitive workforce. Comparing the achievement scores of high school graduates of different states no longer provides as much information as comparisons of the scores of graduates in major nations of the world. While high school graduates in other major nations of the world perform well on the international educational measures, most American students fare poorly. This performance must change.

Because demographic data indicates that the workforce in our nation will be more diverse in the coming years. Naisbitt's statement becomes a guiding force for business education.

Business educators are preparing students to compete in a global society. Seventy-five percent of the today's information did not exist twenty years ago; eighty percent of today's information will be replaced in the next five years. The amount of available information doubles every six years, and the projection for the year 2010 is that the amount of available information will double every thirty-seven days.

Indeed, the information age is here. This is an era in which knowledge has overtaken steel, oil, and wheat as a source and measure of wealth and strength. Knight, chief of National Economic Management of the World Bank, stated in the Sunday, February 19, 1989, edition of *The Seattle Times, Seattle Post Intelligence* that information technology is the most fundamental revolutionary force in the world today.

To continue to teach in the traditional mode and to require courses as stipulated in the past does not seem to be the way to go. Business educators must teach students how to learn. Educators must teach students to listen and to respond adequately. Students must be taught to come up with creative solutions to problems and to develop self-esteem. Students must be capable of setting goals and have the motivation to achieve. Students must have personal career development plans and interpersonal and negotiation skills. Students must be organized and be able to work in teams and to motivate others.

Narrow vocational education, adjusted to the needs of the moment, is made obsolete by changing technology. Vocations have multiplied beyond the schools' abilities to accommodate them. What is needed is education for change not for static job competencies. Business education should start at the elementary level and continue throughout the entire educational process. Business education is the most viable way to educate for our changing workplace.

Business education has certainly been affected by technology and will be affected by technology in the future. At the same time, the present factory-based model of education is not working.

Educators accustomed to acting as knowledge dispensers must instead act as curriculum strategists and classroom coaches. They must guide students toward discovering answers with computers rather than merely providing them with information and testing their recall.

When studying business education, students learn the relationships of one facet of business to another. They understand how the functional areas of business, such as marketing, management, accounting, production, and finance must work together in a successful business. In addition, they learn the basic skills of computation, communication, decision making, and problem solving. After studying such business processes as markup and markdown, determining the interest on a loan, and figuring the present value of a debt instrument, students readily understand how computational skills are used and why they are important. They also see that jobs are lost, work is not properly completed, and orders are not received because of poor communication; consequently, the skills of writing, listening, and speaking are important components of all business education courses.

LUCILLE KORNEGAY

REVIEW OF LITERATURE

Needs and Motivation

A need can be defined as a "biological or psychological requirement; a state of deprivation that motivates a person to take action towards a goal" (Darley, Glucksberg, and Kinchla 1990, 743). Our needs are seldom satisfied completely and perfectly; improvement is always possible. People are thus motivated by their needs or by the tensions the needs create. Their behavior can be seen as movement toward goals they believe will help satisfy their needs. Look at one very influential humanistic theory of motivation that deals with this central concept.

Maslow's Hierarchy: Abraham Maslow has had a great impact on psychology in general and on the psychology of motivation in particular. Maslow (1970) suggested that humans have a hierarchy of needs. Lower level needs for survival and safety are most essential. All people require food, air, water, and shelter; all seek freedom from danger. These needs determine behavior until they are met, but once people are physically comfortable and secure, they are stimulated to fulfill needs on the next level—the social needs of belonging, love, and self-esteem. When these needs are more or less satisfied, people turn to the higher-level needs of intellectual achievement and, finally, self-actualization. Self-actualization is Maslow's term for self-fulfillment, the realization of personal potential.

Maslow (1970) called the four lower level needs—survival, safety, belonging, and self-esteem—deficiency needs. When these needs are not met, motivation increases to find ways of satisfying them. When they are satisfied, the motivation for fulfilling them decreases. Maslow has labeled the three higher-level needs—intellectual achievement, aesthetic appreciation, and self-actualization—being needs. When these needs are met, a person's motivation does not cease; instead, it increases to seek further fulfillment. For example, the more successful people are in their efforts to know and understand, the harder they are likely to strive for even greater knowledge and understanding. So, unlike the deficiency needs, the being needs can never be completely fulfilled. The motivation to achieve them is endlessly renewed.

Maslow's theory has been criticized for the very obvious reason that people do not always behave as the theory predicts. Most people move back and forth among different types of needs and may even be motivated by many different needs at the same time. Some people deny themselves safety or friendship in order to achieve knowledge, understanding, or greater self-esteem.

Criticisms aside, Maslow's theory does provide a way of looking at the whole person, a person whose physical, emotional, and intellectual needs are all interrelated. This perspective has important implications for education. Students who come to school hungry, sick, or hurt are unlikely to be motivated to seek knowledge and understanding. A child whose feeling of safety and sense of belonging are threatened by divorce may have little interest in learning to divide fractions. If the classroom is a fearful, unpredictable place, and students seldom know where they stand, they are likely to be more concerned with security and less with learning. Maslow's hierarchy can also provide other insights into students' behavior. Students' desires to fulfill lower level needs may at times conflict with a teacher's desire to have them achieve higher-level goals. Belonging to a social group and maintaining self-esteem within that group, for example, are important roles for students. If doing what the teacher says conflicts with group rules, students may choose to ignore the teacher's wishes or even defy the teacher.

A great deal has been written about needs and motivation. For teaching, the most fully developed and relevant work involves the need to achieve.

David McClelland and John Atkinson were among the first to concentrate on the study of achievement motivation (McClelland, Atkinson, Clark, and Lowell 1953). People who strive for excellence in a field for the sake of achieving and not for some reward are considered to have a high need for achievement.

Lessons for Teachers: All people need to feel safe, secure, accepted, competent, and effective. Some people may have developed a particularly strong need to achieve. Most people are motivated when they are involved with tasks that give them a sense of progress towards achievement. No one enjoys failure, and for some people it is crushing. People are unlikely to stick with tasks they have difficulty performing or respond well to people who make them feel insecure or incompetent and cause them to fail.

Maslow's theory can suggest ways to plan activities that meet students' needs to increase motivation. Remember that the lower level needs must be met before the higher level needs can become motivating. To make students feel safer and more secure with difficult material, educators might organize extra tutoring sessions (Wlodkowski 1981). They may also create psychologically safer class environment: wrong answers and mistakes can become occasions for learning, for probing the thinking behind the answers, instead of occasions for criticism (Clifford 1990 1991). Needs for belonging and self-esteem might be met in part by allowing students to work in teams.

Since needs for achievement vary from one student to another and from one situation to another, it may help to know where students stand when planning activities. Which students, for instance, have high achievement needs? Which students have achievement needs, and which students are primarily motivated by a need to avoid failure. Those students who are highly motivated to achieve are likely to respond well to challenging assignments, strict grading, corrective feedback, new or unusual problems, and the chance to try again. But for those students who wish to avoid failure, less challenging assignments, ample reinforcement, small steps for each task, lenient grading, and protection from embarrassment are probably more successful strategies.

Discovery Learning

Jerome Bruner's early research on thinking (Bruner, Goodnow, and Austin 1956) stirred his interest in educational approaches that encourage the development of thinking. This interest led Bruner to write several books on teaching and learning, including *The Process of Education* (1960), *Toward a Theory of Instruction* (1966), and *The Relevance of Education* (1971). In these books, Bruner emphasized the importance of understanding the structure of a subject being studied, the need for active learning to make personal discoveries the basis for true understanding, and the value of inductive reasoning in learning.

Structure and Discovery: Subject structure refers to the fundamental ideas, relationships, or patterns of the field—that is, the essential information. Structure does not include specific facts or details about a diagram, set of principles, or formula. Many of the tables and figures in Bruner's text attempt to communicate the structure of key ideas in educational psychology, for example, the different kinds of reinforcement schedules (Table 6.1, 207) or the process of learning and forgetting in long-term memory (Figure 7.22, 243). According to Bruner, learning will be more meaningful, useful, and memorable for students if they focus on understanding the structure of the subject being studied. For example, if students learn the concepts for figure, plane, simple, closed, quadrilateral, isosceles, scalene, equilateral, and right, they will be on their way to understanding one aspect of geometry. If they can place the terms into a coding system, they will have a better understanding of the basic structure of this part of geometry and how these terms relate to one another.

A coding system is a hierarchy of related concepts. At the top of the coding system is the most general concept, in this case, a plane, simple closed figure. More specific concepts are arranged under the general concept.

In order to grasp the structure of information, Bruner believes, students must be active—they must identify key principles for themselves rather than simply accept a teacher's explanations. He believes teachers should provide problem situations that stimulate students to question, explore, and experiment. This process has been called discovery learning. In discovery learning, the teacher presents examples, and the students work with the examples until they discover the interrelationships—the subject's structure.

Piaget's Theory of Cognitive Development

During the past half century, the Swiss psychologist Jean Piaget devised a model that describes how humans go about making sense of their world by gathering and organizing information (Piaget 1954, 1963, 1970). Piaget's ideas will be examined closely, because they provide an explanation of the development of thinking from infancy to adulthood.

According to Piaget (1954), certain ways of thinking that are quite simple for an adult are not so simple for a child. Sometimes all a teacher needs to do to teach a new concept is to give a student a few basic facts as background. At other times, however, all the background facts in the world are useless. The student simply is not ready to learn the concept. With some students, a teacher will discuss the general causes of civil wars and then ask why they think the American Civil War broke out in 1861. But suppose the students respond with the question, "When is 1861?" Obviously their concept of time is different from the teacher's. They may think, for example, that they will someday catch up to a sibling in age, or they may confuse the past with the future.

Influences on Development: Cognitive development is much more than the addition of new facts and ideas to an existing store of information. According to Piaget, the thinking process changes radically, though slowly, from birth to maturity. Why do these changes occur? Underlying Piaget's theory is the assumption that people constantly strive to make sense of the world. How do they do that? Piaget identified four factors—biological maturation, activity, social experiences, and equilibration—that interact to influence changes in thinking (Piaget 1970). Most developmental theories include maturation, activity, and experience, which are briefly examined here.

One of the most important influences on the way people make sense of the world is maturation, the unfolding of the biological changes that are genetically programmed in each human being at conception. Parents and teachers have little impact on this aspect of cognitive development.

Activity is another influence. With physical maturation comes the increasing ability to act on the environment and learn from it. When a young child's coordination is reasonably developed, for example, the child may discover principles about balance and experiment with a seesaw. So, as people act on the environment—as they explore, test, observe, and eventually organize information—they are likely to alter their thinking processes at the same time.

As people develop, they also interact with the people around them. According to Piaget, cognitive development is influenced by social transmission or learning from others. Without social transmission, people would need to reinvent all the knowledge already offered by our culture. The amount people can learn from social transmission varies according to their stage of cognitive development.

Maturation, activity, and social transmission all work together to influence cognitive development, but how do people respond to these influences?

Basic Tendencies in Thinking: As a result of this early research in biology, Piaget concluded that all species inherit two basic tendencies, or "invariant functions." The first of these tendencies is toward organization—the combining, arranging, recombining, and rearranging of behaviors and thoughts into coherent systems. The second tendency is toward adaptation or adjusting to the environment.

Organization: According to Piaget, people are born with a tendency to organize their thinking processes into psychological structures. These psychological structures are their systems for understanding and interacting with the world. Simple structures are continually combined and coordinated to become more sophisticated and, thus, more effective. Very young infants, for example, can either look at an object or grasp it when it comes in contact with their hands. They cannot coordinate looking and grasping at the same time. As they develop, however, infants organize these two separate behavioral structures into a coordinated higher-level structure of looking at, reaching for, and grasping the object. They can, of course, still use each structure separately (Ginsburg and Opper 1999).

Piaget gave a special name to these structures. In his theory, they are called schemes. Schemes are the basic building bocks for thinking. They are organized systems of action or thoughts that allow people to represent mentally or "think about" the objects and events in the world. Schemes may be very small and specific—the sucking-through-a-straw scheme or the recognizing-a-rose scheme, for example. Or schemes might be larger and more general—the drinking scheme or the categorizing plants scheme. As a person's thinking processes become more organized and new schemes develop, behavior also become more sophisticated and better suited to the environment.

Adaptation: In addition to the tendency to organize their psychological structures, people also inherit the tendency to adapt to their environment. Piaget believed that from the moment of birth, a person begins to look for ways to adapt more satisfactorily. Two basic processes are involved in adaptation: assimilation and accommodation.

Assimilation takes place when people use their existing schemes to make sense of events in their world. Assimilation involves trying to understand something new by fitting it into what is already known. At times, people may have to distort the new information to make it fit. For example, the first time many children see a skunk, they call it "kitty." They try to match the new experience with an existing scheme for identifying animals.

Accommodation occurs when a person must change existing schemes to respond to a new situation. If data cannot be made to fit any existing schemes, then more appropriate structures must be developed. People adjust their thinking to fit the new information instead of adjusting the information to fit their thinking. Children demonstrate accommodation when they add the scheme for recognizing skunks to the scheme for identifying animals.

People adapt to their increasingly complex environments by using existing schemes whenever these schemes work (assimilation) and by modifying and adding to their schemes when something new is needed (accommodation). In fact, both processes are required most of the time. Even using an established pattern such as sucking through a straw may require some accommodation if the straw is of a different size or length than the type the person is used to using. People who have tried to drink juice from a box package, know they have to add a new skill to their sucking scheme—not squeezing the box or juice will be forced through the straw and straight up into the air. Whenever new experiences are assimilated into an existing scheme, the scheme is enlarged and changed somewhat, so assimilation also involves some accommodation.

There are also times when neither assimilation nor accommodation is used. If people encounter something that is too unfamiliar, they may ignore it. Experience is filtered to fit the kind of thinking a person is doing at a given time. For example, if a person overhears a conversation in a foreign language, he or she probably will not try to make sense of the exchange unless he or she has some knowledge of the language.

Equilibration: According to Piaget, organizing, assimilating, and accommodating can be seen as a kind of complex balance. Piaget assumed that people continually test the adequacy of their thinking processes in order to achieve the balance.

Briefly, the process of equilibration works like this. If people apply a particular scheme to an event or situation and the scheme works, then equilibrium exists. If the scheme does not produce a satisfying result, then disequilibrium exists, and people become uncomfortable, which motivates them to keep searching for a solution through assimilation and accommodation. Thus, their thinking changes, and they move ahead. In order to maintain the balance between our schemes for understanding the world and the data the world provides, people continually assimilate new information by using existing schemes and accommodating their thinking whenever unsuccessful attempts to assimilate produce disequilibrium.

Technology/Experiential

Scully (1987) agrees that one of education's greatest achievements will be the ability to incorporate technology into the process of learning so that students can learn in the way they learn best, individually. Students should be able to pace themselves at their own rate. Why should teachers have to bring the whole class down to the lowest common denominator? Students have the possibility to pace themselves in their education through using the personal computer. In the area of computer applications, business educators can become the experts. They can team up with educators in other disciplines and show them the many uses for which the computer can be used to educate students.

In the October 1989 edition of *Personal Computing*, O'Malley indicated that the revolution was yet to come. He further stated that marching students and teachers from one conventional classroom to another in locked-step schedules does not foster the new ways of learning.

John Dewey, the great American philosopher, warned against ignoring the effect of technological and scientific change on human values.

Dewey's theories about learning through practical experience are supported by cognitive research that shows students learn better when they solve real-life problems as opposed to being drilled on irrelevant bits of information. As a result, many schools are trying to reorganize curriculum and instruction to incorporate "authentic learning"—the new term for learning by doing.

Technology, some experts say, can contribute greatly to the active, experiential learning that Dewey advocated many years ago.

Computers, and the information technologies based on them, may be the most versatile development in education since schools themselves. As teaching devices, they can feed information to students with efficiency far beyond that of textbooks and classroom lectures. As management tools, they can help to monitor students' progress, ensure that those who need extra help receive it before their grades suffer, and ease virtually all the administrative tasks required of any complex organization. And, as communications systems, computers can give educators access to the latest in educational research and foster their professional growth (Thomas and Knezak 1991).

With existing computers and telecommunications equipment, a student can search vast databases or collect weather data and share it online with scientists and students at other sites. A pupil doing a research project on a planned landfill site can create a multimedia report—text, graphics, sound, and video—and present it to a community group or store it for other students to use as a resource.

In the year 2000, desktop computers are harnessing the power of supercomputers. Advances in digitization have made it possible to transfer data at lightning speed and to combine text, sound, and video images to create multimedia environments.

The information superhighway allows rapid transfer of text, voice, and images along fiber optic lines. Communications, cable television, and entertainment companies are currently forming strategic alliances to make use of this superhighway.

The future holds out even more possibilities thanks to advances in computer chip design and fiber optic technologies. The power of information technology is doubling every few years. Currently, home entertainment uses are the focus of attention; however, once established, the educational applications are enormous. Students could easily tour Versailles electronically, browse the vast holdings of the Library of Congress, or swap e-mail with a scientist.

Students can often feel isolated in a classroom. They often think an instructor may not care as much about the students as the subject matter. Few teachers have the time or opportunity to make personal contact with every student every day. E-mail offers a forum for one-on-one communication as frequently as the instructor or student wishes. Students frequently describe e-mail as being more personal and more convenient than other types of communication.

Educators agree that all of these technological innovations will promote radical changes in teaching and learning if they get online.

Yet, desks are still arranged in rows, teachers lecture more often than not, and textbooks serve as a defacto curriculum. Consequently, computers and other technologies sometimes have reinforced the present, antiquated educational practices.

Technology has a powerful role to play in creating conditions for authentic learning, but only in concert with people changing their minds about education. Making good use of computers requires a wide variety of skills which are different from those needed in conventional teaching and school administration. Educators today may be called on to work with word processing, spreadsheet, and database software; evaluate computer-based programs; plan new facilities; select appropriate computer hardware and software; and apply for grants to pay for it. Only the youngest and luckiest educators had the chance to work with computers during their professional training. The rest have a great deal of learning to do before the success of educational computing is assured.

While the probable impact of future developments in information processing and communications is being debated, existing technologies already are playing an important supporting role in promoting authentic learning.

Peakview Elementary School in Cherry Creek, Colorado, is a recently built restructured school that is taking advantage of multimedia applications. Students routinely use computers to prepare multimedia projects for presentation, according to Karen Peterson, technology coordinator for the school, and the presentations sometimes stored in a computer-based student library where other students can use them as resources.

Rapid technological progress in telecommunications, information technologies, and advanced manufacturing technologies have caused a revolution in the workplace. To function in offices and factories in the global environment, all workers need to know vast quantities of specialized information that is available through fiber-optic networks at the touch of a few keystrokes. The opportunities to stimulate the human senses through multimedia are endless. What will these developments mean for schools?

As schools tap into these new capacities, some experts predict, the curriculum is bound to become more fluid and personalized. In the old order, classrooms depended heavily on textbooks, printed predigested documents that are reviewed by adoption committees and then serve for years as the main classroom tool until they are replaced. In the future, some experts say, single mega sources such as textbooks will fade in influence as learners scan vast electronic resources to find the information they need. Educators will not have a predigested curriculum; instead, what may replace it is a living, student-created curriculum. The curricular possibilities for creating authentic learning experiences are virtually limitless.

As the sources of information expand dramatically, the challenge of gathering information quickly and usefully to pursue a learning activity grows. This fundamental fact is bound to cause a revolution in working life. To function in offices and factories in the global environment, all workers need to know how to use technology to produce products or manipulate information. Our nation's schools must get on line.

The prevailing belief is that teachers are not willing to accept and use the new technology. Teachers, according to some, are incorrigible *technophobes* who have an almost superstitious fear that one day they will be replaced by the computer.

Another challenge for business educators is to take the lead and inspire other teachers to become advocates for change by asking school districts to give them the opportunity to discover what technology can do for them.

It is amazing that a huge number of teachers are making and finding the time to do experiments with new technologies and really enjoying it. These pioneers have embraced technology, not as an end in itself, but because they believe technology can extend their reach, empower their students, and inspire creativity.

So, as we educators look at technology and alternative methods to solve the problems in schools, and as they attempt to reform school systems to take advantage of research and technological advancements, it serves them well to look back at the great educational theoretician, John Dewey. In his lecture, "Experience and Education," he sought the golden means in the solution of educational issues.

Traditional education, he said, is based on the following assumption:

The subject-matter of education consists of bodies of information and of skills that have been worked out of the past; therefore, the chief business of the school is to transmit them to the new generation. In the past, there have also been developed standards and rules of conduct; moral training consists in forming habits of action in conformity with these rules and standards. Finally, the general pattern of school organization (by which I mean relations of pupils to one another and to the teachers) constitutes the school as a kind of institution sharply marked off from other social institutions. (Dewey 1938).

Those who were in favor of the progressive school criticized the type of education that was viewed as the imposition of knowledge from above and from outside. It imposed adult standards, subject matter, and methods upon those who were growing slowly toward maturity and, thus, did violence to their experience.

Imposition from above is opposed expression and cultivation of individuality; to external discipline is opposed free activity; to learning from texts and teachers, learning through experience; to acquisition of isolated skills and techniques by drills is opposed acquisition of them as means of attaining ends which make direct vital appeal; to preparation for a more or less remote future is opposed making the most of the opportunities of present life; to static aims and materials is opposed acquaintance with a changing world. (Dewey 1938)

Dewey resolved the conflict between traditional and progressive education by reference to the nature of experience and its full implications for education. The traditionalists erred, he believed, because of indifference to the relationship between the knowledge, skills, and techniques they would have the child acquire and his inner attitudes and dispositions. The progressives, despite their concern for the inner life of the individual, his interests, felt needs, and desires, tended to ignore the two-fold nature of experience: the fact that the quality of experience derives from the interaction between environment and internal conditions. Learning through experience, as an educational objective, thus requires attention to environmental factors (subject matter and activities carefully planned) in relation to the personal needs, desires, purposes, and capacities of the student (Dewey 1938).

In Dewey's lecture, "The Way Out of Educational Confusion," he dealt with the advocates of liberal and cultural education and those favoring the introduction of practical and vocational subjects in the curriculum. This dispute, Dewey indicated, resulted in part from the phenomenal increase in knowledge, together with recent trends toward interrelationships between fields once separate and distinct, and in part from developments within modern society that had so saturated the arts and technologies. Thus, he concluded that new organizations and new syntheses of subject matter were needed which would both liberalize practical and vocational education and relate more meaningfully the cultural and humanistic subjects with "the interest and activities in which the mass of men and women must perforce engage." (Dewey 1931)

Finally, as educators continue to look for solutions to current educational issues, they must realize that the technological revolution has arrived, and they must take advantage of new technology. Computers are a source of information and feedback that helps students to create and evaluate their own ways of solving practical problems, and even to model the results of putting them to use. In this way, computers free students to develop analytical and creative abilities that are required for any productive role in the modern world, but which are all but ignored by traditional teaching methods.

HISTORICAL BACKGROUND

Throughout its history in American public schools, business education has been influenced by wars, technological development, research, economic and sociological factors, legislation, financial sources, and regulatory agencies. Technological developments have given impetus to research and legislation, research and legislation have furthered technological development, and all three have interacted with other social and economic developments.

The invention of the typewriter, along with the war, precipitated increased demand for clerical workers and the employment of women in offices.

Three collective forces contributed to the drive toward economic growth and security in America, which has resulted in a business-oriented society characterized by high achievement in the production of wealth and the creation of power. In the process, the human factor has been considered largely in terms of its contributions to such achievements.

History further shows how revisions in methods of production, office facilitation, and product distribution have brought change in job requirements for office work and in education essential to job success.

Software on retailers' shelves, computerized telephone sales, and personalized mass mailing, among other developments, have awakened the world to the impact of technology on the office. Word processing classes sprouted in high schools, colleges, and industry training programs. Educators responded to advances in office technology by attempting to instill skills that would help students to secure jobs in a rapidly changing market.

The invention that had the greatest impact on the business office in terms of the increased need for clerical workers was the typewriter. Also, it was the basic function and operation of the typewriter that was instituted in today's computers and word processors.

Office machines covered in this research project are confined to electronic data processing equipment and related office machines used in the area of business operations.

Although the historical events that triggered more recent developments in electronics are noted, this research report deals with the background for these recent developments.

Concern has been expressed that the technological developments are affecting training of office workers. Before business educators can know which area to examine, it is essential that knowledge be gained of the equipment in use and the actual experiences of business in transferring and retraining employees for work with electronic systems. Also, it is important to determine any changing patterns in office employment so adjustments in preparation may be made.

Definition of Terms

The following terms are defined:

Office: The office is an information processing place, not a vital decision-making place. The function of he office is supportive. It supports the work of managers (the decision makers) and vital functions of an organization such as manufacturing, marketing, personnel administration, and finance.

Physically, an office may be a desk and a file in a corner of a room, or it may be an entire building, depending on the size of the organization. In either situation, the office is where data are manufactured into management and customer information and where records are maintained so that the operations of the group being served can be directed and developed.

Clerical Workers: Those who specialize in office work are generally known as clerks. The function of clerks in an organization is clearly understood to be different from that of managers or factory workers. It is widely understood that an office clerk keeps records, accounts, and correspondence and uses a typewriter, adding or calculating machines, and, recently, electronic data processing equipment. Because of the continued increase in the number of employees who come within this occupational classification, the word clerk, like many generic words of wide application, has become an indefinite term and needs to be clarified. Clarification is achieved by adding descriptive words to clerk or by substituting special job titles that indicate the level, scope, or type of clerical work performed, for example, file clerk, mailroom clerk, data-processing clerk, clerk typist, stenographer, receptionist, correspondent, and accountant.

Automation: Automation in an office is the process of handling the clerical operations of a business with little human intervention once the data have been entered into the system.

Data Processing: Data processing is the handling of all the paperwork that results from the production and distribution of goods and services.

Integrated Data Processing: The system of office machinery that employs a common language is known as integrated data processing tape or punched cards, which can be read and produced by many machines.

Electronic Data Processing: Electronic data processing is the handling of the basic clerical functions—classifying, sorting, summarizing, recording, and computing—by machines, which control the flow of electric current and whose operating components are vacuum tubes or transistors.

Computers: The term computers is used to refer to the entire electronic data processing system.

The following job categories changed drastically as a result of new technology: senior and junior accounting clerk, bookkeeping machine operator, general clerk, payroll clerk, senior and junior tabulating machine operator, senior and junior keypunch operator, executive secretary, secretary, stenographer, and senior and junior typist.

History of Machines

Four studies were helpful in doing this research (1) *Business Machines* (Morse 1932), (2) *Office Automation* (Brown 1955), (3) *Office Automation Applications* (Brown 1957), and (4) *The Introduction of Office Machines and Employment of Office Workers in the United States*, 1901-1950 (Harms 1955).

Each of these studies was similar in that the researchers studied one phase of the development of office machinery. Both the Morse and the Harms studies predated the launching of electronic data processing for business applications. Morse traced the development of office machines from Pascal (in France, 1642) to the first automatic typewriter marketed in 1926.

The Harms study presented the introduction of office machines as related to their dollar value. The stock of office machines for the period was presented in 1947 constant dollars, indicating a 1400 percent increase in the stock value of office machines during the first half of the century.

Both of Brown's studies related to electronic developments. *The Office Automation* publication was concerned with keeping readers informed of the latest developments in the field of electronic data processing by means of updating bulletins and office automation applications comprising a group of case studies of users of electronic data processing.

Technological Development

Although development of the present-day electronic computers can be directly traced to Babbage's analytical engine, 1822, the first business application is credited to Hollerith, a statistician chief clerk in the United States Census Office, who developed an electrically operated punch card sorter. Actually, it can be said that the electronic digital computer is an outgrowth of research done during World War II, since the computer designed from 1939 to 1946 resulted in electronic devices that calculated at lightning speeds, a necessary parameter for solving ballistic problems. Because of the astonishing results, efforts were made to determine other uses for these computer systems.

So far as systems for handling business applications are concerned, the first fully automatic system, UNIVAC I, entered the commercial market in 1951. Since that time, eleven large-scale systems and twelve medium-scale systems, and five small-scale automatic computer systems have entered the market. Overall, the number of users of large-scale equipment increased from one in 1951 to 311 in 1958; medium-scale users, from three in 1952 to 1,586 in 1958; and small-scale automatic equipment users from none in 1931 to 210 in 1958. In addition, 1, 343 nonautomatic, small-scale users were busily engaged with business applications in 1958, and these had also grown.

Acceleration of the computer movement began in 1953 and reached a peak in 1955. It continued with the introduction of new models at a somewhat slower rate.

Major changes over the period involved:
1. Increased speed of computations, which can be noted by the speeds of the Mark I (1944) compared with those of the IBM 705 (1955).
2. Reduction in the size of the unit. Accomplishments in the area of size have been achieved through using transistors instead of vacuum tubes in the construction of the computers. Other important advantages of using transistors to manufacture the equipment include lower air conditioning requirements and reduced power costs.
3. Expansion of internal storage (filing facilities). Mark II's internal storage capacity was 100 words; the IBM 705's internal storage capacity expanded to nine hundred thousand words.
4. Increased speed of output. Many of the computers have automatic printers, which produce six hundred lines of 130 characters a minute.
5. Built-in checks to signal the operator when the computer locates an error.
6. Reduction of access time. Strides made in reducing access time have resulted in the ability of the machines to handle continuous accounting, which means that each transaction can be recorded as it takes place, with the necessary adjustment made to each account involved.
7. Improved methods of input. Developments in the area of data input involve the use of sensing equipment. Through optical character sensing and magnetic character sensing, input is accomplished automatically, which results in faster and more accurate input.
8. Special purpose equipment used for industries where problems unique to their work occur. Among those industries using special purpose equipment are banking, transportation (airline reservations), retailing, and inventory control in the manufacturing industry.

Applications: Not even the area of computer development moved as rapidly as that of application. From the strictly scientific applications of the 1940s, the computers have been programmed for virtually every known business processing application, namely, accounts receivable and payable, banking, order-invoice, payroll, inventory, order and sales statistics, general accounting, expense accounting, cost accounting, production control, labor distribution, property accounting, commission computation, and policyholders' records. The first application in the business field involved the handling of records of policyholders by insurance companies, but payroll is generally conceded to be the most popular business application programmed to large, medium, or small-scale systems.

Trends in Office Employment: Close to four million clerical workers represented about 8 percent of the 1930 labor force. From 1930 to 1950, office workers increase 64 percent, or 42 percent faster than the population. Growth of office machine operators during the period led with 305 percent; stenographers, typists, and secretaries increased 101 percent, and accountants and auditors increased 98 percent. A slower rate of growth prevailed among bookkeepers and cashiers, with 30 percent, but this increase was still 7 percent greater than the growth in the civilian labor force.

The United States Bureau of Labor Statistics employment figures revealed that total employment increased 25 percent during the 1930 to 1950 decades while that of the selected office occupations increased 68 percent, more than twice as much as total employment. Within the clerical occupations selected for study, employment in all occupations, except those of bookkeeper and cashier, increased by more than 50 percent; office machine operators outstripped all other categories by jumping 310 percent. It is significant to note here that when the office machine operators were traced to industries, the three industries employing the larger proportions in 1950 were finance, insurance, and real estate; public administration; and manufacturing.

In 1930 these selected office occupations accounted for about 8 percent of total employment, and they rose to more than 10 percent by 1950. If the clerical categories not included in this study (agents, library attendants and assistants, physicians' and dentists' attendants, transportation baggagemen, bill collectors, vehicle dispatchers and starters, express messengers and rail clerks, telegraph messengers and operators, and station ticket and express agents) were added, clerical employees in 1950 would have comprised 14 percent of all employed workers. All office employment statistics, except those of office machine operators, followed this trend. In that one exception, male office machine operators, 7.8 percent, paralleled the decrease among female operators.

The conclusion emerges that the development of electronic data processing did not grow out of the need for some means to halt the ever-increasing office employment figures, nor did it grow out of a desire to reduce office costs. It did, however, parallel the economic movement and came about as a fortuitous innovation, which was immediately grasped as a possible solution to the office dilemma. The fact that electronic data processing equipment became commercially available at the close of the Korean War, just as the economy was gearing itself for increased production, was accidental. There is no evidence that this new technology was an outgrowth of the needs of business; rather, there is strong evidence to support the theory that scientific and engineer technological improvements in electronic equipment permitted the development of the equipment for business applications.

Implications for the Future: While installations of electronic data processing equipment are increasing, office personnel will be rearranging themselves into occupational categories that are quite different from those of the clerical workers defined in the beginning of this historical sketch. Five general groups of office workers are emerging as groups essential to the electronic offices.
1. Systems Manager: the person directly responsible for all operations of the electronic data processing system, including planning and coordinating work of all personnel.
2. Programming Staff: a group of workers comprised of a chief and assistants who plan and execute all programming operations, including preparation of flow charts, coding information for programming, and supervision of file of programming materials.
3. Operations Group: technicians who operate the computer and those who operate the peripheral equipment. These operators are charged with the responsibility of wiring plugboards, supervising the staffs, and maintaining detailed records of time devoted to performance of each job.
4. Input Group: a work group comprised of typists and keypunch operators, who transcribe all of the data to be fed into the electronic system. To this group belongs the responsibility for accuracy of all input data.
5. Records Group: the people responsible for maintaining tapes, punched cards, punched paper tapes; controlling outgoing and incoming tapes and cards; maintaining records concerning the use of the tapes and cards; and preparing new cards when damage from use occurs.

Layoffs will probably occur among office workers with outdated skills, understanding, and knowledge and workers who are not sufficiently qualified to be retrained for upgraded jobs. Another form of displacement, attrition, will affect those high school graduates and non-high school graduates who are not trained with the adequate skills or knowledge to permit them to assume places in either of these five occupational categories or I those groups completely unaffected by electronic data processing, such as secretaries, stenographers, or typists.

With this historical perspective concerning the business office, we can see the correlation that exists today and the need to prepare competent individuals for the electronic office and for the global *information highway.*

CHANGING NEEDS AND REFORMS

THE REFORM MOVEMENT

Schools Must Get "online": Here's a way to know whether technology is really working in schools: Ask kids what they're doing in class. If they say, "I'm using a computer," the system isn't working. If they say, "I'm doing my math or science on a computer," then the approach is successful. With that observation, Sam Whiteside, a sixth grade teacher in Santa Rosa, California, puts educational technology in the proper perspective.

Computers, videodiscs, videocassette recorders—all the fancy hardware and software often lumped together under the term *educational technology*—represent nothing more than tools to enhance teaching and learning. Without ready and willing teachers to use computers, technology can accomplish nothing.

The Nation-At-Risk Report, published in 1983, had a great impact on business education. The purpose of the report was to improve education at all levels. To enhance this improvement, recommendations were made at the high school level to increase high school requirements. The recommendations educators refer to as Chapters Five and Six had an enormous impact on business education in the state of Pennsylvania because it required:

four years of English	three years of social studies
three years of math	one/half year of computer science
three years of science	

two years of a foreign language for college-bound students.

The mandate resulted in a decrease in the number of classes that could be taken as electives.

Virtually every state adopted some part of this report, and the number of high school students enrolled in business classes decreased. Now with the requirement of 21.5 credits for high school graduates, students have only five electives available to them.

Almost ten years after the Nation-At-Risk Report and five years after the implementation of the report, college entrance tests remain virtually unchanged, and what has happened to the 50 to 60 percent of the students who do not go to college? (Incidentally the Nation-At-Risk Report was written primarily for the college-bound student).

Nearly a decade of reform has produced virtually no improvement in the quality of education. (Lauro Cavazos November 1990)

Business educators have always dealt with information. Sixty-five percent of the labor force is employed in information processing positions, among them: programmers, secretaries, managers, lawyers, clergy, newspaper reporters, teachers, accountants, insurance people, bankers, librarians, clerks, stockbrokers, bureaucrats, technicians, engineers, etc. By the end of this century more than 85 percent of the labor force will be employed in information processing. The title of this discipline indicates the content that must be taught or other areas will provide instruction in the business information domain.

Business teachers are preparing students to compete in a global society. Seventy-five percent of today's information did not exist twenty years ago; 80 percent of today's information will be replaced in the next five years. The amount of available information doubles every six years, and the projection for the year 2010 is that the amount of available information will double every thirty-seven days.

Teaching the Basics and Establishing Criteria: Business teachers must continue to deal with the whole person in general education. They must include the fundamental processes that will improve basic business skills, including oral and written communication skills.

Business teachers have done very well with setting up requirements and credits, but they need to be more flexible with respect to those inputs and processes, particularly in the elimination of the one hundred twenty clock-hour rule for defining high school credits and in the elimination of a specific number of courses in specific subject areas as graduation requirements. What matters is what students know and can demonstrate, not how many credits they accumulate. To this end, educators must begin preparing students to meet the Twenty-first Century challenge for students who are capable of competing in a global society.

According to *The Wall Street Journal*, February 9, 1990, "Jobs are becoming more demanding, more complex, but our schools don't seem to be up to the task. They are producing students who lack the skills that business so desperately needs to compete in today's global economy, and in doing so they are condemning students to a life devoid of meaningful employment."

The article continued by stating that corporations are having to retrain students so that their employees can meet job standards. The *Journal* further reported that in an international study of thirteen year olds, the United States ranked last in math proficiency, and South Korea ranked first.

To continue to teach as teachers have in the past and to require the same courses as school systems in the past does not seem to be the way to go. Business educators must teach students how to learn. They must teach students to listen and to respond adequately. They must teach students to come up with creative solutions to problems. They must teach students to develop self-esteem. Students must be capable of setting goals and have the motivation to achieve. They must have personal career development plans and interpersonal and negotiation skills. They must be organized, able to work in teams, and able to motivate others.

Counselors do well in explaining to students how to go from high school to college, but educators must also help students make a smooth transition from high school to work. Schools must send the best students to the best jobs.

Indeed, the information age is here. This era is one in which knowledge has overtaken steel, oil, and wheat as a source and measure of wealth and strength. Knight, chief of the National Economic Management of the World Bank, stated in the Sunday, February 19, 1989, edition of the *Seattle Times, Seattle Post Intelligence* that "Information Technology is the most fundamental Revolutionary force in the world today."

PERSONAL INQUIRIES

Keyboarding will be used as an example or model for using a different approach to teach the subject along with the fundamental processes. A personal inquiry into a class follows.

The instructional goal was to instill in students the importance of a positive attitude toward their future, their peers, and their community while learning a very valuable skill.

Self-esteem was enhanced in the classes by using the following strategies:
1. praising a specific task;
2. actively listening to the students;
3. accepting students' opinions;
4. allowing students to express their feelings;
5. asking students for their opinions on how to solve problems;
6. encouraging students to share experiences;
7. students acknowledging their own errors;
6. saying to the student, "You are right"' and
9 promoting firm handshakes and smiles.

An interdisciplinary approach was used within the classroom, which reinforced the basic skills and placed specific emphasis on language arts.

Reading, writing, and arithmetic are basic tools of learning and are essential to the mastery of any subject. Business subjects are no exception. In order to teach business subjects successfully, educators must incorporate the basic tools of learning.

There is no doubt about the need to teach reading in keyboarding classes. First there is the stroke response level, when the beginning student sees, thinks, and keys each individual letter on the keyboard. Next there is the word level, when the beginning student learns to combine strokes into words. Finally, students must be able to combine these two levels of reading and apply them to difficult words and combinations as they learn to key sentences.

The ability to understand directions is another area in the teaching of keyboarding in which the teaching of reading is essential. From the beginning, business teachers impress upon students that directions are as important as the keyboarding skill. Students are also shown that it is wise to read directions and then go over them step by step as they present themselves in the problem—thus the process.

The keyboard encourages more and longer compositions and also improves the quality of such work.

The following instructional activities helped accomplish the interdisciplinary approach to teaching the course objectives.

1. Students were given an opportunity to research, key, and print reports on education, science, history, sports, politics, and entertainment.
2. Students participated in a guided research project to find the source of famous quotations. (Library use was encouraged.)
3. Students were encouraged to use the dictionary for communication drills on word division, spelling, and decisions on word usage—cite, site, and sight, for example.
4. Students were also encouraged to compose at the keyboard and their final project was the production of a class newspaper.
5. Students kept journals, and their main portfolios were kept on their personal data disk.
6. All classwork and additional information concerning projects were stored on personal data disks.

A form was developed on which students evaluated themselves, guided, of course by an instructional approach to the ten course objectives set forth at the beginning of the school year:

1. Use the touch system to keyboard information.
2. Correctly use vocabulary related to keyboarding input and information retrieval.
3. Compose usable text at the keyboard.
4. Prepare personal notes, letters, and reports through the use of word processing software.
5. Follow oral and written directions.
6. Develop a positive attitude.
7. Use correct procedures to save and retrieve information.
8. Key information at a satisfactory rate.
9. Proofread so that any keyboarded errors are noted and corrected.
10. Improve attendance and behavior.

It was noted that students were motivated to work at a level consistent with their perceptions of self-competency, which may have been enhanced by teacher expectations. There was a consistent correlation between high ratings on positive attitudes and overall high ratings.

The findings in this research study were made through day-to-day contact with students. The teachers observed their approaches to various tasks as well as their personal interactions, comments, and written compositions.

The students in the Motivation Charter and Service Program were both enthusiastic about keyboarding and really displayed a desire to learn the touch system, but it was soon very obvious that some students, in both groups, were not willing to use the correct techniques that were necessary for success in the course. They did not use the touch system to keyboard at an acceptable rate of speed. In both groups, many cover-ups were used to get around using the correct techniques. This approach was frustrating to the keyboarding teachers, and they wondered how severe the grading process should be for students who refused to use correct techniques.

In questioning and observing these students, they would openly admit and defend their lack of using correct techniques.

Some excuses given for not wanting to use the correct touch techniques were:

"We do not plan to be secretaries."

"Why are correct techniques so important?"

"We know many adults who use only two fingers when keyboarding."

To get proper counseling for students who plan to enroll in keyboarding classes in the future, teachers must inform counselors, directors, and others involved in rostering students to keyboarding that many workers besides secretarial and administrative support employees need to use keyboarding to function effectively in their jobs. These workers include the production manager, who uses the computer terminal to locate specific documents; the inventory assistant, who keeps track of shipments of stock and receipts of new items via the computer terminal; the airline agent, who uses the computer terminal for reservations, passenger check-ins, and seat arrangements; and the business executive, who uses a computer terminal to access current information that is useful in making managerial decisions. Keyboarding has become a primary skill in many vocations, a secondary skill in others, and important in the conduct of personal business by all.

When questioning students, there was one other problem that may have contributed to their poor techniques—they were usually exposed to keyboards at the elementary and middle school levels or earlier. Business teachers, who are experts in the principles of keyboarding skill development and in procedures for instructing others in the skill, are not always employed at this level; therefore, when students enter high school, they have already acquired many poor techniques. This issue prompts a recommendation for business teacher certification at the elementary level."

Because cooperative learning techniques were used, the class was divided into four groups. Teachers had an opportunity to see the students in a less formal classroom atmosphere. Students in each group were assigned a manager, who kept a record of assignments completed by students in the group.

Students were also asked to list their career goals. The following is a list of career goals from the two charters.

Motivation Charter (College Bound)	Service Program (Non-college Bound)
attorney	optometrist
actuary	computer programmer
real estate broker	stockbroker
pediatrician	composer
obstetrician	teacher
engineer	psychologist
federal judge	secretary
professional basketball player	engineer
entrepreneur	entrepreneur
psychologist	physical therapist
medical doctor	obstetrician

communications professional recording artist
executive secretary government service
accountant lawyer

As noted in the above list, there was no significant difference in the career goals for the two classes compared. The Service Program students (non-college bound) had the same goals and aspirations as the Motivation Charter students (college bound), and both groups met the course objectives equally as well.

It was noted that the classification of students may just be another effort used by the school system to create a dichotomy. This report does not suggest that this distinction is intentional on the part of the school system; it merely suggests that more research needs to be done in the area of classifying students as college bound or non-college bound.

Further, many believe that schools create dichotomies in many ways—the unhappiness with homogenous grouping is evident when college-bound high school students are cheated out of experiences in home economics, fine arts, and other vocational subjects and students considered non-college bound are often denied adequate counseling and guidance as well as the so-called formal learning courses.

The problem before educators as indicated in this research report, is to make all education relevant. The emphasis in education, therefore, must be on the learning end of the continuum not on the teaching end. The aim of education must increasingly become the development of inquiring minds.

Teachers certainly wish to be considered specialists in their areas, and they must continue to do research that will have an impact on the future of education. Hopefully, as teachers continue to believe that they can make a difference, they will be empowered to look at and report on classroom research.

Cooperative Learning—Another Approach to Learning

When students plan and work together, they develop cognitively as well as socially. Studies show that this approach leads to greater student achievement. It also increases self-esteem, attendance, and the ability to work effectively with others. Working in a group improves students speaking and listening skills as they articulate their own opinions, debate issues, and make judgments.

In such settings, students become more active learners. They learn to encourage, help, and provide constant feedback to one another. They complement one another's strengths. They learn to trust, depend on, and open up to one another.

For group work to be effective, experience on the part of the teacher to identify students who can bring out the best in one another and experience on the part of the students to develop a cohesive team is paramount. In this way, students will learn to function not only when a competitive and individual effort is needed but also when a cooperative spirit is needed.

Based on the above parameters, a cooperative atmosphere was created in information processing classes.

Mastery teaching, which emphasizes planning by objectives and improving teachers' presentation skills, is based on the psychological principles that have been universally accepted and emphasizes the checking for understanding that is crucial for learning. Davidson and O'leary (1990) identified three well-known cooperative learning structures.

1. Think Pair Share. In this structure, the teacher poses questions to the students in the class, who are sitting in pairs. They think of responses individually, and then they think of a paired response. Then, teachers ask the students to share their agreed-upon answers with the rest of the class.
2. Coop Coop. This highly structured version of cooperative learning includes team building, team topic selection, mini topic selection, preparation of team presentations, team presentations, and, finally, evaluations.
3. The Jigsaw Method. This method includes a task division. Tasks are divided into several parts. Group members are give a topic in which to become experts. Students who have the same topic meet in expert groups to discuss the topics, master them, and plan how to teach them. Students return to original groups and teach what they have learned in their groups. Finally, a quiz is taken and teams are recognized.

In the mastery learning and cooperative learning processes, the teacher is not a solo performer and practice master. The teacher is a conductor of a choir or a orchestra of cooperative learning groups.

Cooperative Learning: The study that follows represents an inquiry into classroom teaching techniques, and the results represent information gained from two classes. The terms information processing, keyboarding, and computer applications are used interchangeably.

The process begins with student interviews concerning their general feelings about school in general and about information processing class in particular and also, their ideas about what they would like to see happen in the process.

Student-Centered Classrooms: The work in the area of student-centered classrooms has been interesting, inspiring, and beneficial to all concerned. It was noted that students did quite a bit of side talk while they were doing their work, but work was completed. It must be remembered, however, that the students were being placed in leadership positions to take responsibility for their own learning, which is what is believed to be the epitome of classroom participation.

The classroom was divided into four groups with about eight students in each group. Leadership was rotated, and, occasionally, an irresponsible leader was chosen or selected by lottery. Because there was more than one leader, usually a stronger leader picked up the work of the weaker leader.

Alternative assessments were also part of the classroom inquiry. Feedback from students about their likes and dislikes of the present grading system (A, B, C, etc.) and suggestions for use of alternative methods was encouraged.

The role played by race, gender, and culture in the classroom, and the influence of these factors on the educational achievement of students has been noted as has the reaction to students (general rapport) and the things left unsaid.

Learning Under a Time-Schedule/Competency-Based method: Students should be allowed to learn at their own pace. Because students learn at varying rates, they may not need the same semester or school year to learn a specific subject.

Experimentation with competency-based instruction in information processing classes proved to be more challenging because students worked at their own pace, which was an outgrowth of being placed in a position of having ninth, tenth, eleventh, and twelfth grade students in the same class. Of course, the students had varying degrees of prior instruction in computer skills and keyboarding; therefore, the privilege of tying all of their previous experiences together to prepare them to be word processors was a challenge. The enrollment was thirty-three students in each class.

Assessment: A summarizing statement concerning the general growth of the students in a particular area allowed for a more comprehensive evaluation of the true progress and growth in a particular subject.

A form was designed to show the daily progress or lack of progress for each student. It also showed the rate of progress in relationship to others in the class. This method was not selected to create competition. It was designed to give the teacher an overall picture of the class and the progress of each student.

Can Teachers Teach Human Relations in the Classroom? Teaching relationships in the classroom were explored because people learn from each other; therefore, complete use of peer counseling, teaching, conflict resolution, and interviews was made.

Research Questions Answered from Data:
Group Projects

1. What are your perceptions or general feelings about school?
2. How do you learn best? (Listening, hands-on experiences, pictures, tests, questions, group work, etc.)
3. Do you think a positive attitude will help you achieve success?
4. Do you have serious career plans?

The above four categories were chosen after reading, analyzing, and interpreting, qualitative data.

The data was reviewed, and four categories were selected for which all of the information received could be summarized. Finally, the group leader from each of the four groups drew the following conclusions from the data:

1. Students overwhelmingly preferred small groups over the traditional classroom setting.
2. Students learned best by seeing and doing—or hands-on experiences.
3. Students had positive attitudes but not enough evidence of self-esteem.
4. With few exceptions, all the students had serious career plans.

Teacher Inquiry Project Plan: The evaluation of the extent to which course objectives were accomplished was done by creating a form on which students evaluated themselves on the ten objectives set forth at the beginning of the course.

The Service Class (non-college bound) was compared with a Motivation Class (college bound) to see what influence previous expectations had on present achievements in keyboarding.

The outcomes were tested by using an interdisciplinary approach within the classes. The fundamental processes were integrated in the keyboarding classes.

Proposed Processes: Students kept a journal in which they wrote down information they acquired that was related to the fundamental processes as well as information that helped them develop positive attitudes. (Example, daily quotations.)

Projection for Using New Classroom Procedures: All teachers should be aware that individual students have different needs and different styles of learning. Teachers must realize that consistent adaptation of instruction and curriculum to individual instructional needs, interests, and abilities is paramount in creating a learning environment that is conducive to learning.

Often, teachers spend all their time on classroom management, and not enough attention is given to adapting instruction to individuals; therefore, the more teachers are able to reflect upon and assess their instructional methods, the more receptive they will become to research and resources for professional growth.

Greater use should be made of school-based professional interaction, also. Realizing that teachers have some concern regarding collaboration, it is still believed that once they realize how much professional collaboration is needed for professional growth, they will rise to the expectations of those who would truly like to see teachers become masters of their profession.

Student-centered classrooms should be based on instructional needs, interests, and abilities. What works in our schools is no longer a matter of opinion, but a matter of knowledge. Teachers must link theory and knowledge to practice and continue to evaluate and reconsider methods of teaching.

School-Based Management

(SBM) School-based Management improves communication among the school's staff and the community. Participation in school budget, curriculum, and staffing decisions gives school personnel the collective opportunity to develop ideas about what is important to emphasize in teaching.

According to Little (1981) the most successful schools are those where school staff members frequently exchange ideas about teaching. SBM opens up communication between parents, teachers, and students. It also improves educational services by giving a larger voice in educational decisions.

Increased authority at the school site may help to attract and retain quality staff. Poor working conditions, including low status and low pay, have made it increasingly difficult to attract bright students to the teaching profession. (McNeil 1987); Nyberg and Farber 1986).

By providing increased discretion and autonomy of objectives to teachers, the role of the teacher may gain increased respect and raise teachers' interest and motivation in teaching.

Many problems may arise in implementing SBM. It may create confusion in role and responsibilities. It may be difficult for teachers, administrators, parents, and students to adapt to new roles, and they may become frustrated if they do not know what is expected of them. (Decker et al. 1977).

For example, principals may not know which decisions must be made in consultation with teachers, which decisions they should make in consultation with parents, and which decisions they should make on their own.

SBM represents a power struggle among administrators, teachers, parents, and students. There are contradictions among central administrators who endorse the philosophy of SBM but find it difficult to allocate decision-making authority to principals who want more control over their own destiny or who are resistant to change. Teachers, parents, and students want greater ownership over objectives, but they do not have the time to spend away from the classroom, their jobs, their families, or their hobbies to develop curricula and perform other administrative duties.

SBM encourages administrators, parents, and school staff to work together on school policy issues; however, it is not necessarily a case of these individuals struggling collectively to obtain greater authority. Teachers may fear that greater parental authority will interfere with their position of power, goals, and objectives.

Many authors speak of the problems in reaching a balance between centralization (Brooke 1984; Decker et al. 1977) It is neither practical nor feasible for a district to develop a fully centralized system of school management. There is a problem in providing too much freedom for school staff and risking confusion and consistency versus the problem of too little freedom and facing a staff that feels restrained or inefficient (Rosenholts 1985).

According to Beaubier and Thayer (1973), "As contrary as it may seem, it is absolutely essential to centralize some aspects of an operation for successful decentralization of the operating unit."

Problems in implementing SBM may arise from the structure of school organizations, such as conflicting state mandates, standardized curricula, or budget and personnel constraints at the district and state level (Duke, Showers, and Imber 1980; Prasch 1984).

Increased involvement of school staff and community members in school policy decisions may conflict with state mandates prescribing curriculum form and content (Darling-Hammond and Berry 1988). For example, the state of Florida has imposed legislative action regarding curriculum standardization, and some districts with SBM programs have requested special status to diverge from state requirements (National School Boards Association 1988).

Although SBM may increase the authority of school personnel regarding budget issues, decisions regarding instructional salaries, the number of teachers, and instructional materials and equipment will be limited by the amount of resources available (Gideonse, Holm, and Sestheimer 1981). In addition, hiring decisions will be limited by enrollment trends, district agreements with teacher unions, and state teacher-student ratio requirements (Johnson 1987).

SBM raises potential conflicts with collective bargaining, for example, by allocating administrative responsibilities to teachers and engaging school staff in decisions that might normally be established by union contracts. As Johnson (1984) suggests, collective bargaining often results in standardization of procedures. SBM, on the other hand, often leads to diversity and differentiation in procedures from school to school. While teachers' unions have traditionally stressed material incentives such as pay raises and benefits, SBM emphasizes ownership over objectives, such as what is taught and what materials are used.

SBM advocates do not believe SBM runs counter to union strategies. In most instances, teachers' unions have not served as obstacles to the implementation of SBM. In school districts such as Date County, Florida, and Hammond, Indiana, the unions have worked cooperatively with the districts to obtain SBM. (National School Boards Associations 1988). In school districts where union leaders have played an important role in the initiation and implementation of SBM, the unions believe that SBM offers a method to move beyond traditional collective bargaining strategies and to acquire the status and autonomy desired by teachers (Casner-Lotto 1988; David 1988; McDonnell and Pascal 1988).

There is a limit to what SBM can do. Although many policymakers advocate the decentralization of authority to the school site, most supporters recognize that SBM alone will not solve all school problems such as low teacher salaries, poorly trained teachers, discipline problems, or societal tensions. Researchers argue that major changes in school effectiveness cannot occur unless educational reforms move beyond a narrow focus on the schools (Carnoy and Levin 1976).

As has been indicated, an important aspect of SBM is its diverse approach to decentralization of various decisions to a variety of key actors. Supporters of SBM warn against assuming there is one best way, rather, they advocate giving individuals at the school site the ability to tailor educational programs to meet specific student needs. The diversity that SBM espouses is at the risk of promising all things to all people without providing a set of guidelines to achieve an effective SBM program. Proponents of SBM contend that it is the increased flexibility that SBM offers which enables school personnel to make better decisions and improve school learning.

There is not a simple blueprint for SBM. A successful SBM program in one school district cannot be copied wholesale and transferred to another district. From past and present experiences, however, researchers have identified several essential ingredients in initiating SBM (Lindelow 1981).

It takes training, gradual transition, financial support, shared goals, and administrators who are willing to share authority and support from the school community. Scholars argue that SBM cannot be imposed on schools; rather, it must acquire the support of the entire school community.

Smaller is Better

American high schools regularly enroll two thousand, three thousand, or four thousand students. The institutions have become enormous.

The excessive growth in our high schools was based on two arguments popularized in the 1950s and 1960s. First, large size supposedly guaranteed an audience for the specialized classes, expensive labs, and diverse extracurricular activities that every good high school was said to require. (This argument is most associated with the well-respected educator James Conant. Ironically, he claimed that a senior class should be only as large as one hundred students to support the desired level of curricular variety.) Second, large schools were believed to provide an economy of scale, but recent research, contrary to the above arguments, has provided strong evidence that big is not only better, it is worse. The research shows, for example, that across the country, dropout rates in high schools with more than two thousand students are twice as high as those of schools with six hundred or fewer students.

Why have large schools failed to keep their promise? In part, only small percentages of students (not more than 12 percent it has been shown) tend to take specialized courses. Also, the large number of extracurricular activities found in large schools is deceptive. There are, in fact, fewer extracurricular opportunities for students on a per-capita basis in large schools than in small ones.

With regard to the supposed economy of scale, most of it results from providing proportionately fewer support staff and extracurricular activities and providing less space for these items; however, these savings also represent costs in terms of dropout rates and poor attendance.

But the great failing of large schools is that they create an unfavorable social climate for learning. When enrollment exceeds five hundred, teachers and administrators no longer know all the students by name, and at one thousand, staff is unable to distinguish an intruder from a student. Students are more remote from staff; they rely on their own friendship circles for support. A strong, shared sense of community does not exist between staff and students or even among students. It is not difficult to understand why destructive student subcultures often emerge.

Research studies document that at-risk students suffer the consequences of large school size most. They are the least likely to capture the rewards that large schools hand out. In large, inner-city schools with high percentages of poor and low achieving students, a culture of poor attendance, class cutting, dropping out, noninvolvement in extracurricular activities, and more threatening acts of vandalism and violence are the norm.

Teachers, of course, confront the effects of a poor social climate in their classrooms and hallways and also in their work with colleagues. A large student body requires a large faculty and more elaborate administrative hierarchy. Teachers are far removed from the decision making that takes place at the top of the hierarchy. The informal means of sharing information, which suffice to keep teachers informed in small schools, are curtailed. Teachers do not see most administrators and other teachers during the course of the day in a large school. They interact mostly with others in their program or department, and a shared sense of school purpose is lost.

Moreover, reducing the size of schools is a prerequisite to educational enterprise, which makes teacher involvement in decision making, more flexible scheduling, the integration of curriculum, etc., so difficult.

The evidence is compelling: smaller schools make effective education more possible. In communities with growing school enrollment, new, smaller secondary school buildings can be built, but what about the thousands of existing huge high school buildings around the country? The most practicable and speedy solution is to divide existing schools into smaller units.

Based on the above research, a qualitative research project within a large comprehensive high school was conducted to see if students felt they were benefiting from an experiment with the charter plan. (Small schools within a school.)

The following questions were asked of approximately one hundred students in grades nine, ten, eleven, and twelve.

SURVEY

Students were told they would be asked to rank their answers on a scale of one to five; five represented the highest score in each category.

1. How do you feel, personally, because you are in a smaller program?
   (Forty-seven percent circled the number four.)

2. Do you feel a smaller program will prepare you better in the courses you are taking?
   (Forty-nine percent circled the number five.)
3. Do you get an opportunity to attend more cultural activities because you are in a small program?
   (Thirty-five percent circled the number four.)
4. Do you have a greater opportunity for extracurricular activities because you are part of a smaller program?
   (Forty-four percent circled the number four.)

It is interesting to note that this survey coincided with some of the statistics that have been discussed concerning charters or small schools within a school.

Analysis of Data Collected (Smaller is Better):

Motivation Students. The purpose was to see how the students felt about their charter, what could be done to better the charter, and how the charter was helping the students to prepare for college and life in general. The students were asked five questions. They were asked to rate each question from one, the lowest score given, to five, the highest score given, and write why they chose that particular rating.

It was observed that the results from each grade were very similar. The results were combined for an overall representation. The data sheet showed the breakdown of each grade to determine a relationship between each question to the actual number of responses. Then the total of all grades and actual responses combined (for each question) was recorded on a table chart. The last table showed the total response percentage for each question with respect to the total number of student responses. In mathematical terms, it was the total number of student responses (for each question) divided by the total number of students multiplied by one hundred. The graphs represented the total percentage of responses (by all students) by the question asked. Each graph represented a different question.

In conclusion, the survey showed that most students felt that the Motivation Program had greatly benefited them. Students who picked low ratings usually felt they were to blame and not the charter.

Data from Survey:

Grade:	Question:	1	2	Responses Actual 3	4	5	Total # of Students Responses:
9	1	2	4	6	23	8	43
	2	0	1	5	15	22	43
	3	2	6	6	21	8	43
	4	2	7	15	12	7	43
	5	0	4	10	4	25	43
10	1	1	3	6	29	14	53
	2	1	2	5	23	22	53
	3	11	4	13	13	12	53
	4	2	1	11	23	16	53
	5	6	8	9	9	21	53
11	1	1	4	5	4	4	18
	2	1	2	2	7	6	18
	3	1	1	5	6	5	18
	4	2	1	5	6	4	18
	5	3	3	3	5	4	18
12	1	0	0	2	7	11	20
	2	0	0	1	4	15	20
	3	1	3	2	7	7	20
	4	1	1	4	8	6	20
	5	2	0	4	2	12	20

Total of all grades combined:

Question	1	2	Responses Total: 3	4	5	Total # of Student Responses:
1	4	11	19	63	37	134
2	2	5	13	49	65	134
3	15	14	26	47	32	134
4	7	10	35	49	33	134
5	11	15	26	20	62	134

Total Percent Chart:

Question:	1	2	Responses Percentage: 3	4	5	Total Percentage:
1	3%	8%	14%	47%	28%	1
2	1%	4%	10%	37%	49%	1.01
3	11%	10%	19%	35%	24%	0.99
4	5%	7%	26%	37%	25%	1
5	8%	11%	19%	15%	46%	0.99

Due to estimation, percentages may be inaccurate by 1%

Each chart represents total number of responses (in %) for each question:

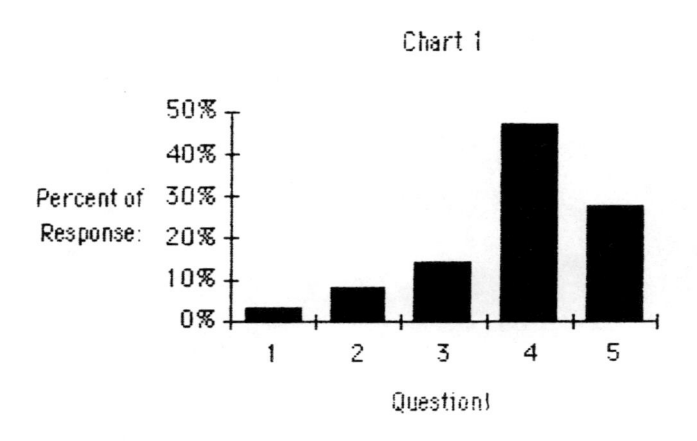

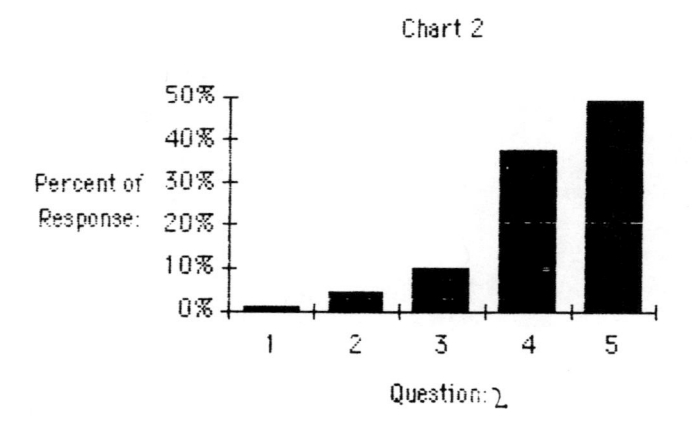

Chart 1

Percent of Response (Question 1):
- 1: ~3%
- 2: ~8%
- 3: ~14%
- 4: ~47%
- 5: ~28%

Chart 2

Percent of Response (Question 2):
- 1: ~1%
- 2: ~4%
- 3: ~10%
- 4: ~37%
- 5: ~48%

Chart 3

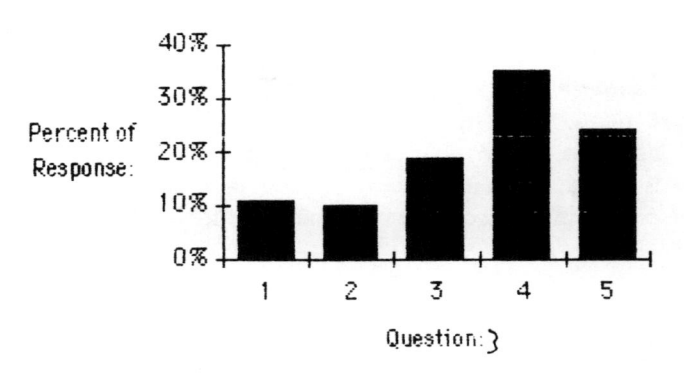

Question: 3

Chart 4

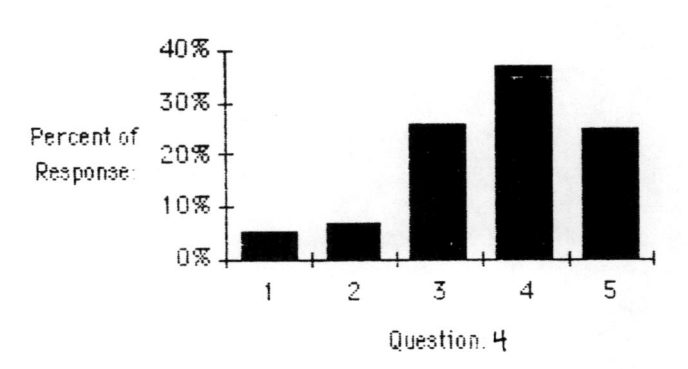

Question: 4

Chart 5

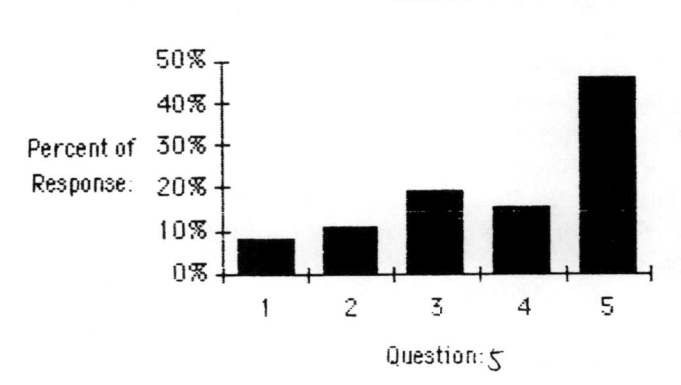

Question: 5

41

LUCILLE KORNEGAY

POLITICAL AND EDUCATIONAL REFORM

Looking at School Reform

School reform is something many people are talking about these days, but what does it mean, and why has it become such a hot topic now? School reform is a general term that refers to a variety of recent efforts to make fundamental changes in the way schools teach children, and it has arisen in response to new social, economic, and technological pressures on society.

The world is changing fast, and the way children are educated to prepare them for that world needs to change as well. At the beginning of the Twenty-first Century, it no longer makes sense to use teaching methods developed in the Nineteenth Century.

The need to reform the schools in the United States is clear. Economic competition from other countries is forcing the United States to become more productive, innovative, and flexible. A highly educated and skilled workforce is needed more than ever before in history. In addition, technology is changing at an explosive rate, making some bodies of knowledge outdated before the textbooks are even off the press.

A more diverse student population has also presented new challenges for educators. Additionally, there is an alarming disparity in the quality of education offered in different school districts. Because this country needs the contributions of all its members to compete in the new global market, it is critical that every child receives an excellent education.

The American public is ready for changes in the schools. In a recent Harris poll, 95 percent of those questioned said the need for reform was "urgent" or "very urgent."

While the need for change is clear, the debate about what changes to make is far from over. Educators, parents, and political and community leaders all over the country have come up with a wide variety of ideas. School reform packages have been proposed by many school districts and states, as well as by the national government.

Some of the more common reform suggestions include:
1. School-based management
2. Small learning communities
3. More parent, community, and business involvement
4. The establishment of national standards of achievement
5. Alternative assessments
6. Professional development schools
7. Greater teacher control of curriculum
8. School accountability
9. Changes in the way education is funded

10. A longer school day/year
11. Broader school choice
12. Developing alternative schools

Schools are already beginning to make significant changes, with many more to come over the next few years. It is quite likely that there will not be one reform blueprint for all schools; rather, each region of the country or each district will choose a course that best suits its needs.

How did America come to commit "unthinking, unilateral educational disarmament," as the Department of Education's attention-grabbing *Nation-at-Risk* report termed it?

The failure of U.S. public education, from kindergarten through high school, is vast and ominous. Myron Magnet made the following observation:

> So ignorant and benighted are many young recruits to the U.S. workforce that one executive after another has recoiled in horror, gasping with astonishment. These are the troops we're supposed to win the global competition with? How can such a workforce dominate the knowledge-intensive industries where the future will be made? What use are modern management techniques that draw on the worker's talents and initiative when he has no dogged, practical Yankee ingenuity to tap? And if two of every five new jobs that the Labor Department expects to be created by the turn of the century will call for more than basic skills, where will the ten million qualified workers come from to fill them. Presumably not all from Hong Kong" (Magnet 1988).

It is believed that not too many people would argue with the fact that the United States has a serious educational problem, but the focus of this report is on a solution, specifically to answer the question whether privatization and educational choice are the best answers to America's educational problem.

Privatization and Choice (a political vehicle for change)

America 2000, an Education Strategy, was the plan of the Bush administration for promoting some of the changes in outlook and organization that the President and the Secretary of Education thought to be the first steps toward better schools. The most controversial part of the plan, of course, was educational choice. Second, privatization was defined, and eight different modes that could be used to achieve it were examined.

Thirdly, highlights of the views of the opponents and proponents of choice were noted. In addition, a school system where a choice has supposedly been implemented successfully was studied. These views were examined based on the needs of the post-industrial society in which these educational strategies would be implemented.

Shortly after becoming Secretary of Education and after a series of White House briefings, Lamar Alexander, with former President George Bush, introduced a thirty-four page document called America 2000, An Education Strategy, which was a plan to jump-start education. Three of the most substantial and innovative parts of this plan follow.

1. National Examinations. World-class standards for what children should know and be able to do would be established in five core subjects: English, mathematics, science, history, and geography. The President proposed a National Education Goals Panel to define those standards and to sponsor national examinations to determine how well U.S. students were performing. These "American Achievement Tests" would be made available for fourth, eighth, and twelfth-grade students in those five core subjects.

2. New American Schools. At his press conference on April 18, 1988, President Bush stated that "the centerpiece of our National Education Strategy is not a program; it's not a test. It's a new challenge to reinvent American education, to design New American Schools for the New Year 2000 and beyond." The President envisioned 535 schools (including one in every Congressional district) that were to be in business by the year 1996. Those 535 schools, amounting to less than half of one percent of the nation's 110,000 public elementary and secondary schools, were to be academic bellwethers—one-of-a-kind, high performance schools," that would break all molds and rethink all traditional curricula and teaching methods. By their achievement and daring, they would show the rest of the public school establishment the way to the heights.

3. Choice. While the American Achievement tests would let parents and voters know how their schools were doing, choice would give them the leverage to act. Such choices would include all schools that served the public and were accountable to public authority regardless of who ran them, to paraphrase Lamar Alexander. America 2000 envisioned two ways of promoting choice. Congress would be asked to revise Chapter One, the largest federal school-aid program, so that federal dollars could "follow the child" to whatever extent state and local policies

permitted. To encourage the states to loosen their restrictions, Congress would also be asked to authorize $200 million in grants to school districts to help them develop school-choice programs that would include both public and private schools. Vouchers were defined as entitlements that could be used to implement educational choices.

What is privatization and what are the ways that it may be implemented? Privatization is transferring activities conducted by public employees to the private sector. The activities transferred may include the funding as well as the actual delivery of services. In this analysis however, the emphasis is on the delivery of educational services. Briefly, below is an explanation of a variety of ways that privatization can be implemented according to Myron Lieberman:

1. The *contracting out* of public services is defined as the contractual utilization of non-governmental entities to provide or help to provide or help to provide public services. Non-governmental entities can be companies, partnerships, individuals, nonprofit organizations, and/or independent contractors, whether for profit or nonprofit. The test is whether the people providing the service are school district employees. If they are, and they are also acting in that capacity, their services are not contracted out.
    Contracting out applies to any activity required to provide education.
2. *Vouchers* are government payments to consumers or on behalf of consumers who may use the payments at any institution approved by the government for the purpose of the voucher. Thus, in both contracting out and vouchers, government pays the service provider.
3. *Load Shedding* refers to government withdrawal from both funding and providing a service. Although there is very little popular support for educational load shedding at this time, Lieberman suggested that support was likely to increase in the future.
4. A *franchise* is an arrangement whereby a private organization is awarded monopoly privileges to provide a service. For example, a school district could allow McDonald's the right to operate the school cafeteria for a stipulated period of time. Unlike vouchers, the consumer does not necessarily use funds provided by the government to pay for the services.
5. *Subsidies* are government payments or credits to producers to minimize or eliminate the costs to service users. In effect, tax exemptions for nonprofit schools are subsidies. Education tax

credits may also be considered to fall within this category of privatization.
6. *Voluntary service* is simply the provision of service by parents or other volunteers. Home schooling and the presence of Planned Parenthood representatives in sex education courses illustrate this form of privatization.
7. The *sale of government assets* is a transfer of property rights to tangible assets from government to the private sector for an agreed upon price.
8. *Leaseback arrangements* are the construction or purchase of public facilities by private parties who then lease the facilities to public agencies under mutually agreed upon terms. An example is a school district that cannot get the voter approval required to build a new school and arranges for private construction—after which the school leases the facility at a rental amount agreed upon prior to construction (Lieberman 1989).

Who are the opponents and proponents of voucher plans? Those groups opposing vouchers include the teacher unions, the American Civil Liberties Union, and various religious denominations. These groups state that studies have demonstrated that private schools enroll a disproportionate number of students from the more affluent groups in our society. Voucher critics base several objections on this fact. One is that a voucher plan would mainly benefit parents who are economically favored. Another is that low-income parents would not be able to afford private schools even with undoubtedly lower tuition, thus reducing or eliminating the voucher's usefulness. In addition, the lack of private schools, especially in the inner city areas, the time and expense of transportation to and from them, and the related school costs would also serve to undermine the utility of vouchers for less affluent parents.

Voucher opponents also assert that private schools would avoid low achievers to bolster school reputation. Inasmuch as disadvantaged minorities include a disproportionate number of low achievers, private schools would tend to avoid both groups. Such an outcome would tend to stigmatize public schools and would have negative consequences for the morale and incentives for their students, parents, and teachers. A great idea of this concern is based on opposition to *tracking*—the practice of grouping students according to aptitude or achievement. Sometimes the term is also applied to grouping students by their educational objectives, such as "non-college bound" or "the college bound." There is concern that vouchers would encourage tracking and have undesirable effects on the tracks that imply less aptitude, lower achievement, or less ambitious educational objectives. Another potential negative is that all students, even of the same age and grade level, are not equally expensive to educate. For example, it usually costs more to educate disabled students than those who are not disabled. Thus, even if the vouchers were related to parental income, private schools would seek those students who were the least expensive to educate; the others would be ignored or relegated to inferior schools.

In short, the objection to vouchers is that under a voucher system, public schools would end up with the disadvantaged, disabled, disruptive, and/or otherwise difficult or expensive-to-educate students. Public education would lose its middle-class support, while private schools would be the beneficiaries of it; public schools would become the "dumping ground" of our educational system. Public schools would continue to exist, but their role as a means of upward mobility and social and racial integration would disappear.

Voucher supporters have responded to these objections in various ways. One way was to frame voucher proposals in ways intended to alleviate the objections. For example, the amount of voucher could not be related to parental income, thereby providing low-income parents with higher vouchers than middle or high-income parents. It has been suggested that parents be prohibited from adding to the voucher. Such prohibitions however, are not likely to be enacted. For one thing, the voucher amounts would have to be very substantial if parents would not add to them, which would probably make the voucher legislation prohibitively expensive and also lead to increased state regulation of voucher schools to enroll a certain proportion of children from low-income families and to avoid increased segregation.

In some instances, voucher supporters rely on a different factual or policy analysis to counter these objections. For instance, schools seeking to establish reputations for high achievement would not ordinarily try to enroll low achievers. It does follow, however, that there would be no competition to enroll the latter and improve their educational achievement.

Similarly, voucher proponents assert that vouchers would facilitate, not foster, racial integration. At this time, there is no feasible way for inner city black parents who want to spend more for better education to do so. They cannot afford private schools; enrolling their children in a better public school would require moving to a more affluent neighborhood, which most would find prohibitive. Yet, by supplementing the voucher from personal income, these parents could improve their children's education. In other words, vouchers would break the connection between residence and school, making it possible for schools to enroll a more racially diverse student body than if students were drawn only from the surrounding neighborhood.

Is there evidence available that choice would make a positive contribution to improving education and expanding productivity in the future? More than thirty states have implemented some type of choice plan or have choice on the legislative agenda. Since Minnesota seems to be leading the nation in expanding parent and student choice, this report will focus on Minnesota.

According to Dave Durenberger (U.S. Senator, Minnesota), in 1988 Minnesota students assumed the right to choose schools outside their own districts, first with permission of their home district, a year later without restriction for districts with more than one thousand students, and in 1991 without restriction for all districts in the state. The first year, 435 students in Minnesota exercised the option to choose their school, in 1989 more than thirty-seven hundred exercised the option.

Durenberger also stated that once Minnesota's Open Enrollment Program was fully implemented, students could be denied enrollment in a nonresident school district only if the district lacked space or would fall out of compliance with racial desegregation guidelines.

The law forbids exclusion of nonresident students because of race or ethnicity, previous academic achievement, athletic or extracurricular ability, handicapping conditions, or previous disciplinary proceedings.

State aid follows the student to his or her chosen district, and the nonresident district must provide transportation from its border to the school selected by nonresident students.

Leading up to this revolutionary change in the rules, Minnesota took several other steps to expand parent and student choice in other ways. Those steps began in 1985 when the Minnesota Legislature began allowing eleventh and twelfth grade students to attend public and private colleges and universities and state vocational schools at public expense. About six thousand students are now participating in this Post-Secondary Options Program.

Perhaps even more important, dozens of school districts have started or expanded new programs for students who might otherwise have left that school district to attend a post-secondary institution.

A third choice option in Minnesota permits students ages twelve to twenty-one, who have not succeeded in one public school, to attend another public school outside their home district.

In 1989, about fourteen hundred students enrolled in the High School Graduation Incentives Program, a number that increased to eighteen hundred in 1990. Many former dropouts were convinced to return to school in a different setting.

A fourth choice option provides year-round high school education in nontraditional settings. According to the Minnesota Department of

Education, approximately six thousand Minnesota students attended school in these Area Learning Centers in the 1989-90 school year.

Finally, approximately five thousand additional students are in an older Interdistrict Transfer Program that allows students to switch districts if both superintendents give their permission.

Altogether, then, more than twenty thousand Minnesota students are participating in one of these five interdistrict choice programs, and that number doesn't count the thousands of Minnesota students who exercise choice within a school district.

What are the implications of educational choice and privatization in the post-industrial society? The wealth of a nation is not its gold, factories, mines, or production machinery. "The foundation of national wealth is really people—the human capital represented by their knowledge, skills, organization, and motivations." (Johnston and Packer 1987). Johnston and Packer go on to state that as the economics of developed nations move further into the post-industrial era, human capital plays an even more important role in their progress. As the society becomes more complex, the amount of education and knowledge needed to make a productive contribution to the economy becomes greater. A century ago, it was thought that factory workers did not need a high school education and that only lawyers or other professionals needed a college degree. Today, a majority of all new jobs require a post-secondary education. Many professions require nearly a decade of study beyond high school, and even the least skilled jobs require a command of reading, thinking, and computing that was once necessary only for the professions. Johnston and Packer continued, "If every child who reaches the age of seventeen between now and the year 2000 could read sophisticated materials, write clearly, speak articulately, and solve complex problems requiring algebra and statistics, the American Economy could easily approach or exceed the 4 percent growth of the boom scenario." This kind of bright future calls for educational standards to be raised considerably. Students must go to school longer, study harder, take more advanced subjects, and pass more difficult tests.

It is believed that some kind of choice or privatization is inevitable, and, to some degree, desirable, but it is evident that many of the proponents of choice are seeking a way to resegregate American schools, maybe as much on the basis of economics as race. Something has to change. The present system for educating America's youths is not working very well, but it has not been shown that the public schools are as bad as Lieberman and others claim they are. There are many good public schools. Perhaps what is really needed is more research and comment on them. As Timothy Healy stated in a *New York Times* review of Lieberman's book, "Mr. Lieberman never talks about the talented people that good schools need, about how personalities mesh to make a school effective, and indeed loved. For those who have taught the young graduates of such schools, their teachers and administrators rise above the narrow bounds of bureaucratic and union rules and have clearly touched the minds and hearts of their pupils."

It seems that the problems America currently faces in education reflect the problems in the larger American society. James Coleman, author of the well-known 1966 Coleman Report on education, observed, "Americans like to think that schools can be used to change society, but the influence goes both ways. from the sixties onward vast social cultural changes twisted schools out of shape. Families grew unstable, what with the increasing divorce rate and in a small sliver of society, an emerging underclass pathology. Schools were never successful with children from families who didn't have a high level of educational aspirations and strong support for those aspirations."

Any plan to jump-start education may prove successful initially. When school systems know they are being scrutinized, they will perform better, but any real and lasting success will come with a new generation of young people. Educators have to wait for a generation of young people whose mothers received proper prenatal and general health care...a generation whose families are united and strong, and where children have been taught that integrity, hard work, caring, sharing, and love are the qualities that make life meaningful...a generation that does not count how many material things can be accumulated in a short period of time...a generation free from the great fear of war so that children believe they will have a future when they mature...a generation that hasn't witnessed so much corruption and deception, and whose leaders will once again be role models.

In the meantime, it is logical to assume that any program that holds teachers, administrators, and others involved in delivering educational services to young people accountable will improve education. The key word is not privatization or choice but ability. A voucher system pushes in the wrong direction. The system inevitably proliferates sectarian schools and so promotes division rather than commonality. It would be justified as a last resort only, if public education were damaged beyond repair, if schools bent on satisfying every interest group developed curricula that were all periphery and had no core, or if children who wanted to learn were prevented from doing so by a disruptive population required to attend school. Most public schools have not reached that point, and the reform movement is likely to keep them from it.

Teacher Preparation and Reform

Prospective educators need foundational knowledge, pedagogical knowledge, advance knowledge, and specialist knowledge. Can a set of principles mediate among these competing claims on the limited time within the education studies curriculum? What should be taught during initial teacher preparation, and what during continuing education, after some experience in the classroom? How could an education school organize and advance this concept.

Situated cognition theory suggests that people learn by indexing new knowledge to situations that cue them as to how to use it. Otherwise it is, as Whitehead said, "inert knowledge," and students don't carry into their school classrooms what they learn on campus. It is recognized that this condition of learning may greatly complicate the faculty's task of agreeing on what and how they teach. How and with whom do they develop the forms for knowledge getting connected to work?

As a possible solution, the Holmes Group came up with the idea of professional development school—housing communities of teachers, teacher candidates, and university professors, all of whom are aggressively inquiring about powerful ideas and exemplifying in their work the intellectual purpose and democratic equity associated with empowerment. (Holmes Group 1990)

Professional Development Schools (a vehicle for reform)

Professional development schools (PDS) are vehicles for reform. They incorporate certain principles—teaching and learning for understanding, communities of learners, inquiry-based practice, and so on—to be carried on in spirit of collaborative egalitarianism; however, a problem arises in the creation of professional development schools. Getting them *on line* becomes the priority, and the spirit of collaborative egalitarianism becomes a secondary concern.

Advantages of a Professional Development School: Pupils get a better education in a PDS, because teachers in these schools are enthusiastic about what they are doing. In addition, the pupils have access to computers and new instructional technology, new curriculum materials, more instructors to help them (including university professors, student teachers, and practicum students), exposure to a larger variety of teaching techniques, and better assessment strategies.

Almost everyone believes schools need reforming, and the PDS is an efficient way to do that. A staff-development program that recognizes teachers will change when the environment of the schools changes and that adds the notion of teacher development as a continuum that begins at the preservice level and continues to retirement is a PDS!

Levine (1988 discussed several important reasons for having professional development schools. First, public schools were established originally to educate many people in basic literacy skills and rote knowledge, but current goals are different; they stress creative and independent thinking and getting students to like classes and themselves enough simply to stay in school. Today's different goals require different school practices and instructional support. The PDS facilitates this change at the school site.

A PDS is analogous to a teaching hospital. It is designed not only to educate novice teachers, but to be a place where university and school faculty can collaborate on research and development—all within an administrative structure that encourages professional development and empowerment. In a PDS, pupils are rewarded with the best possible education. The ideal PDS is a school where teachers and researchers generate new knowledge about education, then put that knowledge into practice as teachers are trained at the cutting-edge of their field.

Stallings and Kowalski (1990) identified six general purposes for a PDS, and all professional development schools address some combination of them. The six purposes are:
1. educating pupils;
2. preparing new teachers;
3. developing innovative teaching practices;
4. conducting research;
5. providing inservice practice; and
6. disseminating educational innovations

Collaboration will improve teaching practice. In 1988, Levine stated that the "same environment which supports the development of knowledge based, inquiry based professional practice is also one which enhances student learning."

Teachers consider field experiences the most important part of their preservice training; however, these experiences often are unstructured and unguided. Better cooperation between schools and universities increases the structure and guidance that prospective teachers receive in the field and increases the value of their field experiences.

To be a self-governing profession, teaching needs a structured induction experience conducted under the supervision of master teachers, who can attest to the competence of new teachers. To Levine, this experience implies the existence of standards of practice, developed and upheld by experienced teachers and required of novices. The PDS can provide this experience.

School-university collaboration can benefit everyone involved. University staff get a laboratory. They get a place to help educate new teachers. They themselves learn more about teaching. Teachers in a PDS get to be on the cutting edge of new methods and materials. The PDS may also take on the role of a staff development center with teachers playing key roles. Teachers get a voice in how future teachers are educated.

More important than special resources may be opportunities to collaborate with other teachers and education professionals from outside the school. Most teachers still tend to work in isolation, but they can be invigorated by meeting regularly with other teachers to compare notes on professional issues and practices. Counterparts at the university or school provide alternative viewpoints. The teacher's job is further professionalized by taking on new roles and responsibilities.

Finally, teachers must be trained in a truly professional environment and this is one of the best ways to have prospective teachers learn theory and merge it with current practices. Also, all teachers must realize the importance of keeping abreast of current changes, and they must be willing and capable of changing with the demands of a new millennium.

Accountability In Education

The word accountability is not widely accepted among educators, but accountability is an aspect that will definitely be needed if teachers are to see improvement in their students; therefore, if teachers are prepared properly for the future, they must then proceed to make themselves accountable.

To achieve these results, the emphasis of this new accountability in education must be on what has been learned. Too frequently, educational managers attempt to explain their activities in terms of resources and processes used rather than learning results achieved. These explanations no longer are adequate. A more sophisticated public is demanding evidence that every Johnny can read, and that he has been provided with the other basic skills necessary to employment and a useful life in an increasingly complex society. The public is demanding product reliability in terms of student capabilities and no longer will accept mere assertions of professional superiority in educational matters. If educational managers wish to retain professional control of the processes in schools, it is axiomatic that those processes must produce the results desired by the public who pays the bills.

In its most basic aspect, the concept of educational accountability is a process designed to ensure that any individual can determine for himself if the schools are producing the results promised. The most public aspect of accountability would be independent accomplishment audits that report educational results in factual, understandable, and meaningful terms. These audits might be undertaken by groups drawn from universities, private enterprise, and state departments of education. They would be employed by local school authorities in a manner similar to the process now employed to secure and utilize fiscal audits. Such audits would serve our educational managers by telling them which educational processes are productive and which are nonproductive and by suggesting alternatives that are likely to be better.

Like most processes that involve a balancing of input and output, educational accountability can be implemented successfully only if educational objectives are clearly stated before instruction starts. One mechanism for ensuring clarity in objectives is the performance contract.

An educational performance contract, as its name implies, would prescribe anticipated learning outcomes in terms of student performance. Unlike contracts that simply describe the work or service to be provided by one party and the payments to be made by the other, the educational performance contract would specify the qualities and attributes of the end product of the service or work performed. In other words, it would establish the quantity and quality of student learning anticipated rather than focus solely on the quality and quantity of effort expended by those providing the work or service.

Performance contracts make greater initial demands on both the purchaser and supplier, but they mitigate most postdelivery haggling because simple performance tests can be used to determine whether or not the product performs as promised.

Conclusion

CURRICULUM INTEGRATION

Curriculum integration is a vision of business education becoming the major player in the integration of all disciplines to better prepare students for the Twenty-first Century.

Business educators think that highly valued knowledge, broad intellectual and vocational skills, and hands-on learning experiences must be taught to all students in school. Given the amount of preparation, revision, and meeting the demands of crisis in education, it is almost impossible for it to be better; it must be different.

Since business education has been considered both academic and vocational because of the nature of its courses, business teachers are in the best position to perpetuate the integration of all disciplines.

The biases and assumptions that led educators to use tracking and divide the secondary school curriculum into academic and vocational halves are at the bottom of current troubles. Facts about current school tracking practices suggest that this division of curriculum has led to the disappointing effects of all education.

The reform movement in education envisioned here would have the goal of providing all students with highly valued and essential knowledge, skills, and attitudes that will enable them to function intelligently as adults in a global and information based Twenty-first Century.

Basically, these fundamental competencies and knowledge might be best thought of as the ability to apply basic, funded knowledge and a well-developed value system to the information based Twenty-first Century.

An emphasis on fundamental process and principles is not a new idea in business education. Late Nineteenth Century advocates, for example, claimed that manual training would complement academic studies in a balanced education. Their argument stressed that students should learn mechanical processes rather than prepare for particular trades and that they should master general principles rather than specific skills. They argued that processes requiring skill with the hands would simultaneously present problems of the mind. Dewey and the progressives later made a similar claim: if students worked with wood, metal, paper, and soil they could achieve alternate and important "ways of knowing." Today, too, many leading business educators call for an integrated curriculum (Silberman 1988). The conception of manual education as relevant and central to the liberal education of all students has never been realized, however prevailing program effectiveness criteria make priorities clear: program content is often assessed for its match with labor-market needs; skill competencies are often measured by employers hiring standards; job placement rates are often the most valued bottom line.

Business educators are challenged to go beyond the call to integrate with academics for specific jobs. With education in the fundamental processes and manual skills, business educators should be leading the reform movement by reconsidering the structure, the curriculum, and the language of business education and, basically, altering the role of comprehensive high schools.

The concept is that business education would become part of the common curriculum in comprehensive schools, which would mean business education would become a legitimate *status knowledge* for all students at all ages. Thus, business education would become a *new basic* and would be subject to the same scrutiny and standards as high-status subjects like mathematics, science, and the humanities.

Reforming business education will require that it be taught to heterogeneous classes. No tracking system or differentiated curricula will achieve the essential purpose providing students with competencies for functioning intelligently in their adult view. The adult world is heterogeneous. Tomorrow's world will demand that people work productively and respectfully with a diverse array of others who share society.

Further, no tracking system can provide an equitable distribution of the integrated curriculum. Current practices indicate if separate business education programs were instituted for college-bound and non-college-bound students, differences in access to knowledge and skills would inevitably result. Placing business education at a common curricular core taught to heterogeneous groups would have other necessary and beneficial effects—it would circumvent the institutionalized labeling and stigma that business students now suffer.

The new and reformed curricula should be centered around essential concepts drawn from philosophy, history, and economics. Business teachers would agree that these three disciplines underline the organization of work, and, therefore, they are appropriate for the basic integrated curriculum. Concepts from philosophy and economics explain how society works; their application results in the economic structures and principles followed in the conduct of production, management, and consumption of goods and services—processes that are at the root of society. Philosophical concepts that suggest how societies can be organized and governed, economic principles that explain how materials, work, and property can be coordinated, distributed, consumed, and exchanged, and historical perspectives on how these principles develop and change can replace current curricula.

Science and mathematics proved a second source for a reformed curriculum. The application of basic knowledge from these disciplines is technology. Technology, including computers, is clearly the focal point of industrial education. These principles govern the properties of materials used in production; they determine the methods used to transform material into goods and services. Broad technology—relevant concepts from the sciences and mathematics—could replace the current emphasis on *industrial education and trades.*

Increasingly, business and industry leaders cite literacy, flexibility, problem-solving skills, and general knowledge as the best preparation for the complex and changing demands of the workplace. The other issue is that of intrinsic value. Students must have a value system. Perhaps even more important than whether employers seek these specific skills is whether curricula, such as those mentioned above, are what society, including educators, most desire for students in comprehensive secondary schools.

There are no easy answers or staff-development programs ready to attack the problem of tracked vocational education. Dramatically altered assumptions aligned with educational research findings and democratic values are required. Just as current practice assures that some students can't or won't learn, schools designed around common curricula and heterogeneity require the belief that all students can and will learn. Curriculum built around organizing concepts and themes will take the forefront in the future.

The special knowledge and skills of business teachers make it logical that they play a central role in the delivery of the courses in the integrated curricula. Such revolutionary change involves major risks. One clear risk is the resistance of business educators themselves, who will be asked to rethink all they have been taught about good business programs. Specifically, the vision and concept offered here will also be resisted by school practitioners and parents.

Realistically, to improve business education and all vocational education, educators must deal with the following critical questions. Whose interests are best served by the focus of programs on preparing students with skills to meet labor-market demands? Whose interests are best served by a focus on developing individuals who can intelligently determine the courses of their own lives with informed decisions about society and their own work within it? In whose interests and toward what ends should business education strive? The answers to these questions will, undoubtedly, lead business educators to reform business education as a concept-based curriculum to be taught commonly to all students in elementary and secondary schools.

In reviewing the skills needed for the work force and workplace future, a variety of educational strategies have been tested in a number of settings. The Carl D. Perkins Vocational and Applied Technology Education Act, Public Law 101-392, has as its basic objective the mandate to assist you in developing the skills for successful transition from school to work. Two key components for this legislation have a direct impact on the way in which business and vocational education develop these skills in students. The first component is the integration of academic and vocational education. With this theme, curriculum development and instructional practices are emphasizing basic skills (English, mathematics, and science) instruction in vocational education classes and developing more applied, real-life learning activities and materials for academic courses. Grubb and his colleagues identified eight basic models of integrating academics with vocational education. These include:

> incorporating academic competencies in vocational courses;

> combining academic vocational teachers to incorporate academic competencies in vocational courses;

> making the academic curriculum more vocationally relevant;

> modifying both academic and vocational education via curriculum alignment between courses and programs;

> developing academies or schools within schools that combine basic academic instruction and technical instruction.

> developing occupational clusters in high schools instead of departments;

> organizing single occupational high schools; and creating career paths or occupational majors (Grubb 1990).

Many of the endeavors to develop these basic skills include the development and use of applied course curricula, including principles of technology, applied communications, applied mathematics, and applied biology and chemistry by the Agency for Instructional Technology (AIT) and Center for Occupational Research and Development (CORD) (Haynes, et al., 1990). In addition, several states and private business firms have developed applied science, mathematics, and language courses to assist with specific regional employment needs related to basic skills.

Instructional practices where academic and vocational teachers collaborate is a hallmark of the integration movement. Teachers sharing concerns, expertise, ideas, and actions have led to a number of positive outcomes, including revitalization, interest development, and real-life learning activities. This educational collaboration has its roots in mirroring the positive influence cooperative work groups have had in business settings. It calls for the teacher to be a model, expert learner, and facilitator of student learning.

The second major component of this legislation deals with the development of Tech Prep programs to assist students in preparing for technical occupations that will require preparation beyond the high school diploma. These programs forge three major partnerships.

1. A partnership between academic and vocational teachers to focus on the integration of rigorous academic content into vocational programs to build basic skills.
2. A partnership between secondary and post-secondary educators to build articulated programs that are efficient and effective.
3. A partnership between business and education to build commitment and support for the programs.

Educators involved with collaborative activities to integrate academic with vocational education and to develop Tech Prep programs must take a more empowered position in leading these educational programs.

EDUCATING WITH A GLOBAL PERSPECTIVE

In September 1989, President George Bush and the nation's governors agreed to six national goals in education, which were to be achieved by the year 2000. Goal number five stated, "Every American will be literate and will possess the knowledge and skills necessary to compete in a global economy and exercise the rights and responsibilities of citizenship." Goal number three stated that American students would leave grades four, eight, and twelve having demonstrated competency in challenging subject matter, including English, mathematics, science, history, and geography; and every school in America would ensure that all students learned to use their minds well so they would be prepared for responsible citizenship, further learning, and productive employment in a modern economy.

The Secretary of Education and the members of the Secretary's Commission on Achieving Necessary Skills issued a report (SCANS) that detailed five workplace "know-how competencies" that schools must teach and students must learn to meet these goals. This report identified "a three-part foundation of skills and personal qualities that lie at the heart of job performance." Basic skills made up one part of the foundation of skills. The commission provided an example of basic skills: reading, writing, listening, and speaking, as well as communications skills, the use of the computer for word processing, graphics, multimedia (video and audio), and manipulation of data bases taught in the context of solving relevant problems.

These identified basic skills need to be taught for students to compete in a global economy; therefore, it is logical to believe that each skill can be taught in a business class.

These skills are taught without the thought that they help prepare students to compete in a global economy. The SCANS report states: "Basic skills find a natural home in English classes." Because the Commission overlooked business education, business educators might ask, 'Why not include these global skills in a business class?' "

To answer the above question, business teachers can teach these basic skills in business education. They must become advocates and let others realize they can teach these global skills.

Students who make up the future workforce must realize they live in a global economy. Through teaching, students need to be encouraged to think about skills, knowledge, and careers in an international setting. Business courses no longer can be taught as though the United States were isolated and independent from the rest of the world. Those days are gone. Whatever is incorporated in business curricula, the subject matters must be taught and learned in the context that the United States but one of many countries doing business, and each country is dependent upon the other for economic survival. This dependency will be successful if members of the workforces in each country understand and appreciate that productivity and cooperation are necessary ingredients in a global economy. Students, as future workers, need to understand this economy to make it happen.

It is critical for business educators to utilize a number of teaching strategies that will enhance students' understanding of change and the change process. Activities should include the use of guest speakers, case studies, and discussions of current events. Students should be given the opportunity to use cooperative learning and alternative assessments and to participate in the implementation of change. Educators should also use learning activities that require students to make prognostications about the future and then identify how they should prepare for such possible events. This effort at forecasting is called *futuring*. *Futuring* examines possible events, both positive and negative, and attempts to identify and assess the possible impact of these events. *Futuring* activities provide students with opportunities to conduct research, work cooperatively with their peers, improve critical thinking abilities, enhance communication skills, and develop problem-solving processes.

Business educators teach students to input, edit, print, file, reproduce, organize, manipulate, and use information to make sound business decisions. Since they prepare workers for every phase in the information cycle, it seems that business education now has the greatest potential for growth since its beginning.

Business education is no longer limited to secretarial training. The increase in the number of information workers brings with it the need for all students to learn to handle information. The structuring of administrative support services in business has changed job requirements and the need for secretarial workers. Business executives now perform their own communications tasks without the assistance of secretaries. All business employees need to be proficient in using electronic mail, composing documents at a computer, and using sophisticated software programs. Business educators predict that significant changes are expected to occur in the business office. The ratio of secretaries to managers is expected to decline. Secretaries will assume more managerial responsibilities, and managers will use computers more to acquire information and make decisions. Business education is the natural vehicle to provide training for all information workers. Instead of losing students, programs, classes, and teachers, business educators should be planning to expand to provide education for all students.

According to Toppe (1991), there is an emerging need for keyboarding as an enabling skill—a tool needed by almost every American worker in all types of companies and at every level in the hierarchy of these companies. Future employees must gain proficiency in the use of the keyboard to enable them to interact with computers. Consequently, business educators need to structure the course to fit the needs of the students—all students.

More than any other facet in the world today, technology presents many challenges and opportunities for business education. Not only do all students need to become technologically literate, all workers, from the factory to the business office need a knowledge of technology. Consumers use technology in the marketplace, and technology regulates people's homes, cars, and communication facilities. Everyone and almost everything is affected in some way by technology.

The study of technology is more than learning a computer software program. The business curriculum should be expanded to teach all students about technology—how to use it, how to learn it, how to solve problems with it, and how to change with it. Technology must be taught as a tool, a tool that changes daily.

Business educators must be ready to take the lead and develop programs as the needs arise. They must be ready to provide the leadership that education so desperately needs.

According to Daggett (1991), the 190s provided the opportunity to make great changes. "Everyone involved in education in the 1990s must be prepared to lead, to follow, or to get out of the way," he said.

EDUCATION AND TECHNOLOGY

The key to successfully adapting to the current technological reality is understanding that innovation is the wellspring of wealth. Technical experience is critical to not only uncovering dramatic breakthrough but to making incremental improvements in products and processes. Access to research and development resources, strong academic institutions, and a highly skilled workforce are essential in this new environment.

Rapid technological progress in telecommunications, information technologies, and advanced manufacturing technologies has caused a revolution in working life. To function in offices and factories in the global environment, all workers need to know how to use technology to produce products or manipulate information. Intricate telecommunication links have radically transformed the way business is conducted, rendering the geographic location of colleagues and clients less relevant. Doing business—sharing conversation and documents—is as easy cross-Pacific as it is cross-town.

Globalization of the world economy has made knowledgeable, skilled, and adaptable people the key foundation of competitiveness for individual businesses and for regions as a whole.

Use of new technology will depend on the workers' abilities to innovate and use technical expertise. Maintaining the flexibility needed to serve specialized markets effectively will require workers who are adaptable and have multiple skills. Selling abroad and monitoring foreign competition will require employees who have knowledge of foreign cultures and who possess sophisticated planning skills and know how to handle information and use communications technology. Education will play a critical role in preparing workers to meet the challenge of technological and organizational change.

The Global Economy: The overarching trend affecting high education at the end of the current millennium will certainly be the reduced probabilities of international conflict and the globalization of the economy. In spite of complaints about de facto barriers to foreign markets, the global playing field is probably more level than ever before. In the new competitive arena, success depends more on the competence of the players than ever before, which inevitably reduces to issues of "human capital." To the extent that educational achievement is an aspect of a competitive workforce, comparing the achievement sources of high school graduates of different states no longer provides as much information as comparisons of the scores of graduates in major nations of the world. In the global economy, the United States high school graduates are competing with high school graduates in Nagaszki and Cologne. United States students, and the rest of the nation for that matter, are not doing as they should in that respect. While America's best high school graduates perform well on the international educational measures, most of the country's students fare badly, a performance that must change. Fortunately, the sector in which America continues to excel is high education, and here lies the competitive edge. This edge must be maintained while concerted actions are taken to improve the quality of education in the public schools.

The Rapidity of Technological Change: Accelerating technological change comprises the second major component for the new education setting. Technological change per se does not. What is the new rate of change? The present emphasis on new materials, information, data processing, new product designs, etc.—all driven by the quickening pace of technological change—argue for both a qualitative and quantitative distinction, which leads some who see and appreciate the connection to label the present stage the "Information Age."

Modern aircraft, transistorized radios, computers, kidney dialysis machines, ultralight sailboats, German and Italian specialty cars, and videodisks describe innovations that increase in number almost more rapidly than lists can be prepared to arrange them or educational and training programs developed to prepare people to fabricate them.

There is little question that this trend will continue and intensify. Technological developments are likely to be more immediately felt in data processing, communications, new materials, and biotechnologies, and their effects will influence conceptions of work place, consumption, and the nature of economic competition.

The technological changes on the horizon suggest that several fundamental changes are under way in the economy. First, technology is gradually overcoming the barriers of time and distance that have organized work through the centuries. In the future, technology will increasingly enable workers to choose where and when they will work. Second, technology is lightening the economy. As products become lighter, more intensively processed, and more durable, the per capita demand for all kinds of materials will decline. Third, technological change is so rapid that it is beyond the capacity of any single firm or nation to manage. Because of technology, the economy of the future will be a race to stay ahead or a race to catch up. Technology will introduce change and turbulence into every industry and every job. In particular, the necessity for constant learning and constant adaptation by workers will be a certain outgrowth of technological innovation.

The call for constant learning and adaptation by workers will be heard again. As for now, the more sophisticated the technology, the more important are human intellect, judgment, and initiative, and the biggest obstacle to installing sophisticated equipment and robots in factories is the scarcity of trained people in the plants.

THE CHALLENGE

Implications for Business Education:

One of the essential skills identified in the U.S. Labor Secretary's Commission on Achieving Necessary Skills (SCANS) report the ability of workers to work with a variety of technologies. This important skill, however, is only one of five competencies identified in the SCANS report. The five competencies considered by the U.S. Department of Labor as essential for preparing young people for work include (1) identifying, organizing, planning, and allocating resources; (2) working with others (interpersonal relationships); (3) acquiring and using information (including computer skills to process information); (4) understanding complex interrelationships (including social, organizational, and technological systems and systems design); and (5) working with a variety of technologies (including selecting and applying the right technology to task) (U.S. Dept. of Labor 1992).

Knowing just information technology, then, won't do the job. Likewise, effective educators must master the information technology area along with a variety of other disciplines such as finance and marketing. Business educators must help students develop the skills with which they can cope and work within a changing environment. Using business subject matter, business programs can contribute to the development of basic skills, thinking and decision-making skills, good interpersonal relationship and communication skills, and personal qualities. Cultural diversity and ethics must be emphasized. As the common phrase goes, students must learn to learn.

It is somewhat ironic that technological changes have actually made many of the traditional business concepts more important. Business educators must make sure that the business curriculum has a proper balance between technology concepts and the basic business concepts in the curriculum. With rapidly changing technology, business educators must examine what they are teaching in the basic business areas and assess its importance for students who will face unparalleled changes.

Technology should force business educators to examine how instruction is being delivered as well as what instruction is delivered. While a considerable amount of emphasis has been placed on identifying the competencies needed for the workplace, much too often educators have not determined the instructional delivery of these competencies. Business educators should be in the forefront of reforming the instructional delivery system.

Cooperative Learning is One Choice! Without question, cooperative learning strategies have been extensively tested, thoroughly researched, and carefully scrutinized. The experts would agree that individualistic and competitive structures have their place in business education, but cooperative structures fill a void that currently exists. Cooperative strategies provide the vehicle to ease the transition from school to work. As business and industry scurry to downsize organizations, eliminate layered bureaucracies, and incorporate more participative management policies, business educators must follow suit. Business teachers are challenged to nurture the interpersonal development, enhance collaborative skills, and encourage the active problem solving and critical thinking that is demanded to function in such an environment. Business educators are challenged to ensure the development of technical literacy but not at the expense of workplace literacy and employability skills. Infusing cooperative strategies into the business education curriculum provides a viable way to accomplish both. Current estimates are that more than 85 percent of the instruction in school consists of lectures, seatwork, or competition, where students are isolated from one another and forbidden to interact.

The social structure within schools is out of line with the social skill needs of a highly flexible technological economy. Though students do not frequently work cooperatively in school, they are expected to do so when they enter the workforce. Without question, cooperative strategies provide one method of initiating a positive change in the reform movement in the classroom.

Challenges of recent educational reform movements have increased pressures on educators to implement more efficient and effective ways to manage the learning environment and facilitate learner outcomes. While educators are struggling with planning and implementing learner-based instruction, managers in the business world are challenged by similar forces The present paradigm shift in education reform was summarized by Daggett and Branigan in 1987: "Present models of teaching do not fit the increasing democratization and on-hierarchical characteristics of an information society." The resultant redefinition of the role of educators as advisors, learning consultants, and facilitators is occurring in the midst of a variety of complex forces, such as increased competition (among school, training agencies, and programs), diminished instructional time, the need for flexibility in instructional scheduling and locations and pressure to educate more learners for less money.

Although educators may not be able to predict the exact future and the impact of technology, they know change will continue at a rapid pace. As with the past decade, computers are getting smaller yet more powerful. Virtual reality and expert systems are predicted to be a major part of the future, and the list of recent innovations continues to grow. Under these circumstances, educating takes on several new dimensions.

Educators cannot wait to see what happens or remain passive. They must be adaptable, flexible, and positive.

Summary

As educators are encouraged to become leaders in the restructuring of schools, they are asked to examine course content, technology, and methodology. Since demographics are changing, teachers must learn to adapt to a changing population with ever increasing social issues that affect their students' willingness and ability to learn.

Business educators must adapt the concept of confluent education, which combines cognitive goals and affective responses, and they must allow students to take responsibility and ownership for their own education. Confluent education, cooperative learning, and outcomes based instruction will provide students and teachers with opportunities to assume leadership roles, improve self-esteem, and develop interpersonal communication skills while focusing on building a knowledge and skills base essential for employment or post-secondary education.

Students must be prepared to adapt to change, to be creative in devising a career plan, and to be flexible as they pursue career goals. Teachers must develop these same qualities in order to facilitate the education of today's students. Teachers must be willing to implement change, create a positive climate for students, and continue learning themselves.

HYPOTHESIS:

>The education of the whole person involves two areas, theory and experience. It is evident from research that students must have hands-on experience that involves them in the process of education; therefore, the more actively students are involved in the learning process and take personal responsibility for their learning outcomes, the greater are the learning results.

PROBLEM:

>How can business educators develop the whole person to reach his or her potential through business technology? The focus will be on helping educators develop the human dimension in their

students as they prepare them to be competent individuals who will become self-educating, lifelong learners.

The dialog involved the keyboarding business technology and a world of ideas—motivation, esteem, etc.

METHOD: The following method used in this research is described as follows:
1. The survey was given to a random group of ninth through twelfth grade Motivation and Service Students. The purpose was to see how the students felt about their charters (small groups) and how the charter was helping the students to prepare for the future.
2. Meaningful questionnaires, which covered pertinent information concerning self-esteem, career goals, and motivation, were given to students in keyboarding classes.

FINDINGS:
1. Students overwhelmingly preferred small learning communities, and their goals and aspirations were the same in both groups—college bound and non-college bound—which justifies the integration of academics and vocational education.
2. Collaboration with all participants—students, teachers, parents, the community, etc.—is paramount for improving student achievement. All must be held accountable and actively involved.
3. Educators must be willing to implement change and be totally committed to the profession.

NEEDED:

Research into the reasons for lack of implementation of technology in the classroom.

BIBLIOGRAPHY

Barram, David J. "Partners for the Nineties: Business and Education." *Educational Horizons,* Summer 1988.

Brann, Ludwig. *Vision: Test-Technologically Enriched Schools of Tomorrow.* Eugene, Ore. The International Society of Technology in Education, October 1990.

Brookhart, S.M., and W.E. Loadman. "Work Perceptions of University and Public School Educators." Paper presented at the annual meeting of the American Educational Research Association. San Francisco: ERIC NO. ED 309 720, 1989.

Brown, Richard Hunt. *Office Automation Applications.* New York: Automation Consultants, Inc., 1957

Bruner, Jerome S. *The Process of Education.* Cambridge: Harvard University Press, 1960

———*The Relevance of Education.* New York: Norton, 1971

"Business Educators Team Up to Motivate High School Students." *The Wall Street Journal,* May 9, 1990.

Carnevale, Anthony P., and Leila J. Gainer. *Workplace Basics: The Skills Employers Want.* American Society for Training Development and U.S. Department of Labor, 1990.

Carnoy, M., and H. Levin. *The Limit of Education Reform.* New York: D. McKay Co. 1976.

Casner-Lotto, J. "Expanding the Teacher's Roles: Hammond's School Improvement Process," Phi Delta Kappan 5, 1988

Cavazos, Lauro. "Building Stronger Bridges From School to Work." *Partnership in Education Journal*, November 1990.

Clifford, M. "Needs and Motivation: Lessons for Teachers" in *Educational Psychology*, 5th ed. Edited by Anita Woolfolk. Boston: Allyn and Bacon, 1990.

Daggett, W.R., et al. "Business Education in the 1990s—A Window of Opportunity." *Strategic Planning for the 1990s, Twenty-Eighth Yearbook*, Reston, Va: National Business Education Association, 1991.

Darley, F., Glucksberg and Kinchla. "Needs and Motivation" in *Educational Psychology*, 5th ed. Edited by Anita E. Woolfolk. Boston: Allyn and Bacon, 1990.

David, J. S. Purkey, and P White. "Restructuring in Progress: Lessons from Pioneering Districts." Paper prepared for the National Governors' Association, Washington, D.C. 1988.

Davidson, Neil, and Pat Wilson O'Leary. "How Cooperative Learning Can Enhance Mastery Teaching." *Educational Leadership*, February 1990.

Davidson, Percy E. *Occupational Trends in the United States, 1870-1930.* Calif.: University Press, 1940.

Decker, E., and Brooke, et al. *Site Management: An Analysis of the Concepts and Fundamental Operational Components Associated With the Delegation of Decision-making Authority and Control of Resources to the School-site Level in the California Public School System.* Sacramento California: State Department of Education, 1984.

Dewey, John. *Experience and Education.* New York: The Macmillian Co., 1938.

———*The Way Out of Educational Confusion.* Cambridge, Mass." Harvard University Press, 1931.

Duke, D., B. Showers, and M. Imber. *Teachers as School Decision Makers.* Standford, California: Institute for Research on Educational Finance and Governance, Stanford University, Project Report No. 80-A7, 1980.

Durenberger, Dave. "Educational Choices and the Generational Impact." *Vital Speeches*, LVI, 1990.

"Educators Predict Swing to Emphasis on New Four C's." *Herald Journal*. Logan, Utah: March 6, 1989, 4.

Fantini, M., and M. Gittell. *Decentralization: Achieving Reform*. New York: Pracger Publishers, 1973.

Fusselman, Kay. "Technology and Women's Employment: The Office of Today and Tomorrow." *The Secretary*, November/December, 1986.

Gideonse, H.D., D. Holm, and P. Westheimer, *School Site Budgeting: Abstracting the Literature*. A Project for the Education Panel of the Cincinnati Association, 1981.

Ginsburg, O. and Opper. "Basic Tendencies in Thinking—Organization" in Jean Piaget's *The Development of Thought: Equilibration of Cognitive Structures*. Translated by Arnold Rosin. New York: Viking Press, 1977, 1988.

Grubb, Norton, Gary Davis, Jeannie Lum, Jane Plihal, and Carol Morgaine, *The Cunning hand, the Cultured mind: Models for integrating vocational and academic education*. Berkeley, Calif. National Center for Research in Vocational Education, July 1990.

Harms, Louis T. *The Introduction of Office Machines and Employment of Office Workers in the United States, 1900-1950*. Unpublished Ph.D. Dissertation. Pennsylvania: University of Pennsylvania, 1960.

Haynes, Thomas. "Defining the Work Force of the 1990s. *National Business Education Yearbook 1992*, 16-17.

Healy, T. "Voucher, Voucher, Who Gets the Voucher?" *New York Times Book Review*, 1989.

Holmes Group *Tomorrow's Schools: Principles for the Design of Professional Development Schools*. East Lansing, Mich. Holmes Group, 1986.

Hosler, Mary. "Incorporating a Global Perspective in Office Procedures." *Business Education Forum*. Virginia: National Business Education Association, Vol. 42, No. 4, April 1992.

Johnson, S.M. *Teachers Unions in Schools.* Philadelphia: Temple University Press, 1984.

―――― "Can Schools Be Reformed at the Bargaining Table?" *Teachers College Record 2,* 1987.

Jones, Gardner M. *Electronics in Business.* East Lansing, Mich. Michigan State University, Bureau of Business and Economic Research, 1958, 94.

Knight, P. "The Practice of School-Based Curriculum Development." *Journal of Curriculum Studies 1,* 1984, 37-38.

Kizzier, Donna, Jody Ford, and Connie Pollard. "Perceived Appropriateness of Technologically Mediated Systems." *Delta Pi Epsilon Journal,* Vol. XXXVI, No. 1, 1994.

Letteri, C. "Teaching Students How to Learn." *Theory Into Practice,* Vol. 24, 1985.

Levine, H.M. *Accelerated Schools for At-risk Students.* New Brunswick, N.J.: Center for Policy Research In Education, Rutgers University, 1988.

Lieberman, Myron. *Privatization and Educational Choice.* New York St. Martin's Press, 1989.

Lindelow, J. "School Based Management" in *School Leadership: Handbook For Survival.* Edited by S.C. Smith, J. Mazzarella, and P.K. Piele. Columbia, Md.: National Committee for Citizens in Education, 1981.

Little, J.W. "The Power of Organizational Setting: School Norms and Staff Development." Paper presented at the Annual Meeting of the American Educational Research Association, Los Angeles, Calif., 1981.

Magnet, Myron. "How to Smarten Up the Schools." *Fortune* 117, 1988, 86-94.

Marburger, C. *One School at a Time: School Based Management, A Process for Change.* Columbia, Md." National Committee for Citizens in Education, 1985.

Marschak, T. and D. Thomason. *Coordination vs. Local Expertise: A New View of School District Decentralization.* Berkeley: School Action Research Center, 1976.

Maslow, Abraham H. *Motivation and Personality.* New York: Harper and Row, 1987.

McClelland, David, et al. "Achievement Needs" in *Educational Psychology*, 5th ed. Edited by Anita E. Woolfolk. Boston: Allyn and Bacon, 1990.

McNeil, L.M. "Exit, Voice and Community: Magnet Teachers' Responses to Standardization." *Educational Policy* 1, 1987.

Mecklelenburger, James A. "Educational Technology is NOT Enough." *Phi Delta Kappan*, September 1990, 104-108.

Meade, Jeff. "Tuning In, Logging On." *Teacher.* Washington, D.C.: Editorial Projects in Education, Inc., January 1991, 30.

Naisbitt, J. and P. Aburdene. *Megatrends 2000: Ten New Directions for the 90s.* New York: William Morrow, 1990.

Nanassy, Louis C., R. Malsbary Dean, Herbert A. Tonne. *Principles and Trends in Business Education.* Indiana: Bobbs-Merrill Educational Publishing, 1977.

National Commission on Excellence in Education. *A Nation At Risk.* Washington, D.C., 1983.

National School Boards Association. *Communicating Change: Working Towards Educational Excellence Through New And Better School District Communication in Public School Educational Operations.* Washington, D.C. 1988.

NBEA Strategic Plan. Reston, Va." National Business Education Association, March 26, 1991.

Nyberg, D. and P. Farber. "Authority in Education." *Teachers College Record* 88, 1986, 4-14.

Oakes, J. *Keeping Track: How Schools Structure Inequality.* New Haven: Yale University Press, 1970.

Odell, L. "Planning Classroom Research" in *Reclaiming the Classroom: Teacher Research as an Agency for Change.* Edited by P. Goswami and Stillman. Cook, 1987.

O'Malley, Christopher. "The Revolution is Yet to Come." *Personal Computing*, October 1989.

O'Neil, Sharon L. "Paradigms for High-Tech Leadership." *National Business Education Yearbook*, 1993, 62.

Participative Management—Decenttralized Decision Making: Working Model, edited by E. Beaubier and A. Thayer. Burlington, Calif." California Association of School Administrators, 1973.

Patton, M.Q. "Analyzing and Interpreting Qualitative Data." *How to Use Qualitative Methods in Evaluation.* Beverly Hills: Sage Publications, 1987

Peterson, P.F., and T. Carpenter. "Using Knowledge of How Students Learn about Mathematics." *Educational Leadership*, Vol. 46, No. 4, 1989.42-46.

"PC Biz: Still Crazy After All These Years." *INFOWORLD*, January 1, 1990, 1-4).

Piaget, Jean. *The Development of Thought; Equilibration of Cognitive Structures.* Translated by Arnold Rosin. New York: Viking Press, 1977.

Powell, A.G., E. Farrar, and D.K. Cohen. *The Shopping Mall High School: Winners and Losers in the Educational Marketplace.* Boston: Houghton Mifflin Company, 1985.

"Powerful Small Computers Ahead." *USA Today*, August 3, 1989, 7B.

Ray, Charles, Janet Palmer, and Amy Wohl. *Office Automation* 2nd ed. Cincinnati: South-Western Publishing Co., 1991.

Reed, Sandra. "Technologies for the 90s." *Personal Computing*, January 1990, 66-69.

Rehbreg, R.A., and E.R. Rosenthal. *Class and Merit in the American High School.* New York: Longman 1978.

Rock, D.A., et al. *Study of Excellence in High School Education: Longitudinal Study, 1980-82—Final Report*. Princeton: Educational Testing Service, 1985.

Rosenbaum, J.E. *Making Inequality: The Hidden Curriculum of High School Tracking*. New York: Wiley, 1976.

———. "Social Implications of Educational Grouping." *Review of Research in Education*. Washington, D.C.: 1985

———. "Track Misperceptions and Frustrated College Plans: An Analysis of the Effects of Tracks and Track Perceptions in the National Longitudinal Study." *Sociology of Education*, 1953, 1980, 74-88.

Rosenholtz, S.J. "Education Reform strategies: Will They Increase Teacher Commitment?" *American Journal of Education*, Vol. 4, 1988.

Rothman, Robert. "Now the Results." *Teacher Magazine* March 1990, 18-20.

Rubens, B.O. "Vocational Education For All In High School?" *Work and the Quality of Life*. Edited by J. O'Toole. Cambridge Mass." MIT Press, 1975.

Sapre, Padmakar M. "Toward a Redefinition of Business Education." *13th Annual Peter L. Agnew Memorial Lecture*. New York University, March 15, 1989.

Schafer, W.E. and C. Olexa. *Tracking and Opportunity*. Scranton, Calif." Chandler, 1971.

Scully, John. "Looking Forward to the 21st Century." *Delta Pi Epsilon Journal* Summer 1987.

Seattle Times/Seattle Post-Intelligence. Sunday, February 19, 1989, A3.

Silberman, H.F. "The Challenge to Vocational Education" in *Education and Work* Edited by H.F. Silberman. (Eighty-first Yearbook of the National Society for the Study of Education. Chicago: University of Chicago Press, 1982

——— *Determining the Goals of Vocational Education*. Columbus, Ohio: The National Center for Researching Vocational Education, 1987.

Slavin, R.E. *Cooperative Learning.* New York: Longman, 1983.

"Smarter Jobs, Dumber Workers, Is That America's Future?" *The Wall Street Journal*, Friday, February 9, 1990, R1.

Solomon, G., D. Prekins, and T. Globerson. "Partners in Cognition—Extending Human Intelligence with Intelligent Technology." *Educational Researchers*, Vol. 20, No. 3, 1991.

Spady, William G. "Organizing for Results: The Basis of Authentic Restructuring and Reform." *Educational Leadership*, 1968, 4-B.

Squires, J.R. "National Study of High School English Programs: A School for All Reasons." *English Journal*, 55, 1966, 282-290.

Stallings, J.A., and T. Kowalski. "Research on Professional Development Schools" in *Handbook of Research on Teacher Education.* Edited by W.R. Huston. New York: Macmillan, 1990

Stern, D., et al. *One Million Hours a Day: Vocational Education in California Public Secondary Schools.* (Report to the California Policy Seminar) Berkeley: University of California, School of education, 1985.

Sternberg, R.J. "Teaching Critical Thinking. Part I: Are We Making Critical Mistakes?" *Kapan*, 67, 1985.

Strassmann, Paul A. "Knowledge Management: Opportunity for the Secretary of the Future." *The Secretary*, June-July 1987.

Taylor, R.E. "Vocational Education." *Encyclopedia of Educational Research*, 5th ed. Vol. 4. New York: The Free Press, 1982, 2002-2012.

Taylor, S.J. and R. Bogdan. "Introduction." *Qualitative Research Methods: The Search for Meanings.* New York: Wiley, 1984.

Thayer, V.T. *Formative Ideas in American Education: From the Colonial Period to the Present.* New York: Dodd, Mead & Co., 1965.

"The '80s Leave a World Defined by PC Explosion." *PC Week* January 1, 1990, 1, 11.

The Governor's Commission on Higher Education. *A Vision for Portland Higher Education*, prepared by the Oregon Independent Colleges Association, May 1989.

Thomas L., and D. Knezek. "School Technology: What Every Educator Must Know" in *Renaissance*, Edited by C. Cetron and M. Gayle. New York: St. Martin's Press, 1991.

Toppe, Judith E. "Keyboarding—An Enabling Skill." *Business Forum*, Vol. 46. December 1991.

Tucker, M., and D. Mandel. "A Voucher Plan for Worker Education." *Education Digest*, 1988, 6-13.

Vanfossen, B.E., J.D. Jones, and J.Z. Spade. "Curriculum Tracking: Causes and Consequences." (Paper presented at the annual meeting of the American Educational Research Association. Chicago: 1985.

White, Betsy. "Do Standardized Tests Help Students? Answer is NO, Teachers Say." *The Atlanta Journal and Constitution*, Sunday, October 29, 1989, A-B.

Wiggs, Linda Henson. "Providing Skills for an Information Society." *Business Education Forum*, Virginia: National Business Education Association, Vol. 46, No. 4, April 1992, 19.

Wlodkowski, J. "Needs and Motivation: Lessons for Teachers" in *Educational Psychology* 5th ed. Edited by Anita E. Woolfolk. Boston: Allyn and Bacon, 1990.

Woolfolk, Anita E. *Educational Psychology*, 5th ed. (Instructors Section prepared by Ruth A. Sandlin and Lynne T. Diaz-Rico, California State University, San Bernardino.) Boston: Allyn and Bacon 1990.